Chapter 1. INTRODUCTION

What is True Religion?

The question today is what is true religion, not what is the true religion. Professor Walid Saif has rightly said, 'the most dangerous division may not be religion versus. religion. Religious freedoms across religious communities or within the same community can be more suppressed by zealous, narrow-minded and exclusivist interpretations of religion.' Christians and Muslims should not argue about which religion is superior, but seek to purge religion of all that is false and inauthentic so that together we grow in our understanding of the truth that God has revealed. Thomas Merton (1915-68), a Trappist monk and influential author, said that the good Christian is not someone who can refute other religions, but one who can affirm the truth in them and then go further.

Let me give an example of how the different emphasis of another religion may make one think more deeply about the subject. I have engaged in conversations with Jews, Christians and Muslims about repentance and forgiveness. Does repentance have to come first? There are passages in the New Testament, such as the parables of the Lost Sheep and the Prodigal Son, which suggest that like the Shepherd or the Father, the injured person may need to take the initiative in seeking reconciliation. But others will say 'How can we forgive someone who is not sorry?' They may also say that that to show kindness to the cruel is to betray their victims

There are other important issues to which we shall return. My point here is that our reflection on them is deepened as Christians and Muslims discuss these great issues together.

This book is not an introduction to Islam in the usual sense, although I hope it will be self-explanatory to those who know little about this religion. Rather it is a reflection on my reading about Islam and my meetings with many Muslims over some forty years. When I first went to India, I was told that the exterior dialogue had to be matched by an interior dialogue. Exterior dialogue is the conversation with people of another faith or the reading about it and the attempt, in this case, to understand what Muslims believe and practice. Inner dialogue is the subsequent reflection, in the light of Christian discipleship, on where there is agreement or disagreement, on where one has questions and on what one can learn. Certainly

Islam has helped to deepen and purify my faith in God. I hope this approach will help Christians understand and enter into conversation with Muslims, although first we may have to unlearn inherited prejudices.

Indeed preparatory reading for this book has made me more aware how prevalent both ignorance of Islam and prejudice against Muslims is in the West. As the then Archbishop of Canterbury, Dr George Carey, said when he addressed Muslim scholars at Al-Azhar University in Cairo, 'It is extraordinary how ignorant we are of one another. Yet ignorance is the most terrible of cultural diseases for from it stem fear, misunderstanding and intolerance.' Some years ago the French Catholic priest and scholar of Islam, Louis Massignon (1883-1962) said that Christians had to accomplish what amounted to a Copernican re-centring in order to understand Islam. It is a task on which we have scarcely begun.

Over one hundred years ago Prime Minister Gladstone, in an attack on the Ottoman Turks, held up in the House of Commons a copy of the Qur'an and declared, 'So long as there is this book, there will be no peace in the world'-although he admitted that he had not read it. As I write the burning of the Qur'an by an American pastor has caused offence and outrage throughout the Muslim world - and indeed some deaths. Prejudice and ignorance is not just on the Christian side. As Dr Ataullah Siddiqui of the Islamic Foundation in Leicestershire points out, the imams and traditional scholars of Islam, who have great influence on Muslim society, are almost unaware of dialogue and their attitudes are shaped by the history of polemical debates.

I hope this book will, at least, help to dispel some of the ignorance and prejudice. This is one reason why I quote quite extensively from both the Qur'an and from Muslim scholars. As Akbar Ahmed, of Cambridge University, 'much depends on those who can build bridges between the two civilisations.'

Yet important as it is to gain correct knowledge of each other's religion, it is I think more exciting and spiritually enriching to talk about our beliefs and devotions rather than just to accumulate 'external' information about a religion. Indeed, it is as I have engaged in discussion with Muslims that the Qur'an has become an alive and absorbing book, whereas on first opening it, without any background, it may seem, like much of the Bible, difficult for a new comer to comprehend.

ISLAM

A CHRISTIAN REFLECTION

Marcus Braybrooke

ISLAM

A CHRISTIAN REFLECTION

To my friends in the Three Faiths Forum

*Humanity! Truly We have created you male and female
and made you to be nations and tribes
in order that you might know each other.
Truly the noblest among you in God's sight
are those who fear Him most.
God knows and observes all*
Surah 49, 13

ISBN 978-1-4717-0087-3

This is a revised version of *What Can We Learn from Islam*
originally published by John Hunt Publishing O-book in 2002.

Some material from *Beacons of the Light*, published by John Hunt Publishing
O-book in 2009 is also included.

ISLAM

A CHRISTIAN REFLECTION

FOREWORD
To the first edition
by
Shaikh Dr M. A. Zaki Badawi

The Rev Marcus Braybrooke is a man of such deep religious faith that he makes us see the divine in every faith and creed. He has devoted a great deal of his energy in the service of the interfaith movement.

Every interfaith organisation in Britain has his name in a place of honour as a member, founder or chairman. His work in building bridges between the communities of different cultural traditions has been exemplary. But it is in his writing that he manifests his warmth and true understanding of the 'Other'. In the present political climate in Europe and the USA, the writings of Marcus Braybrooke are acts of courage inspired by his unbounded humanity and fellow feelings for all humankind. This volume is a scholar's presentation of Islam to the West by a westerner. He outlines those areas of agreements as well as those in which our faiths differ. He took great care in consulting references in order to dispel some of the misinterpretations of Islam. His sympathetic approach should alert the western reader to look afresh into a greatly maligned faith. He writes about Islam with the humility of the seeker of the truth.

Do not the title of the book and its beautifully written contents underline the outstanding quality of the book and its author? I hope that this example will inspire a Muslim to write on what we Muslims can learn from Christians

27th June 2002.

ISLAM

A CHRISTIAN REFLECTION

CONTENTS

Chapter 2. GOD

'I bear witness that there is no god but God ...' The opening words of the *Shahada* or first 'Pillar of Islam.' express the essential message of Islam.

The beauty of the Taj Mahal is overwhelming. I had, of course, seen pictures of it, but when, as a young student, I first went to Agra and saw the Taj, I had a feeling of awe and wonder at the grandeur of God. Made of shining white marble the Taj was built by Emperor Shah Jehan in memory of his beloved wife Mumtaz Mahal. Rabindranath Tagore described as 'a tear on the face of eternity'. When, later, I visited the great Dome of the Rock in the old city of Jerusalem, I had a similar feeling. The Mosque of Omar, as it is also known is built on the place where traditionally Abraham had tried to sacrifice his son Isaac/Ishmael and from where the Prophet Muhammad set out for his ascent to the seventh heaven (Sura 17, 1). It is magnificent with its carpets and ornamentation and uplifting with its sense of space. Whenever I have returned to these buildings, which I have done many times, something of the first experience has been renewed. I have never doubted that Islam is a genuine revelation of God.

Such experiences of the numinous were called *mysterium tremendum* by the theologian Rudolf Otto (1869-1937) in his book *The Idea of the Holy*. The *tremendum* implies a sense of fear and awe and of awareness of our creaturliness, as we are overpowered by the glory of God. There is a sense also of Mystery, which is a feeling of fascination and attraction, which can lead into a sense of joy and peace.

It has been said that 'A God comprehended is no God'. The great mosques of Islam renew in me the sense of the holiness of God, to whom the prophet Isaiah in his vision heard the seraphs call out, 'Holy, holy, holy is the Lord Almighty, the whole earth is full of his glory' (Isaiah 6, 3). This is reinforced by the regular bowing of the head to the ground in prayer.

We believe in the same God

Christians and Muslims largely agree on their belief about God. In 1076 Pope Gregory VII wrote to Prince al-Nasir, 'There is a charity which we owe to each other more than the other peoples because we recognise and confess one sole God, although in different ways.' In 1734 George Sale, a translator of the Qur'an, referred in his introduction to the views of an Italian scholar, Ludovico Marracci, who was the confessor to Pope Innocent XI. Sale wrote:

'That both Mohammed and those among his followers who are reckoned orthodox, had and continue to have just and true notions of God and his attributes (always excepting their obstinate and impious rejection of the Trinity), appears so plain from the Koran itself and all the Mohammedan divines, that it would be loss of time to refute those who suppose the God of Mohammed to be different from the true God...'

More recently, the Second Vatican Council declared that
'God's saving will also embraces those who acknowledge the Creator, and among them especially the Muslims, who profess the faith of Abraham and together with us adore the one God, the Merciful One, who will judge men on the Last Day.'

Even so, this is by no means obvious to many Christians and it *is* necessary to lose time to affirm this point.. Not long ago, I was asked in a BBC interview, 'How can you join with members of other faiths in prayer? Surely, they worship different gods?' My answer was that I am a monotheist and believe there is only one God, who is the Creator of all people. Our pictures of that God may differ, but there is only one Divine reality.

For this reason, as I am writing in English, I prefer to use the word God rather than Allah, to emphasise that there is one Divine Reality of whom we as Christians or Muslims are both speaking, just as I dislike the use of the word 'Yahweh' for God in some modern translations of the Bible. I am aware, however, that Muslims have usually preferred to use the word 'Allah' rather than God in their translations of the Qur'an into English and I honour this when I quote from the Holy Qur'an. 'Allah', of course, is the word that Arab-speaking Christians also use for God.

Both the Bible and Qur'an affirm and declare the reality of God. They do not argue for God's existence. In both, God speaks to human beings or is the object of their praise or the One to whom they pray. Both Christians and Muslims believe that God is One, although some Muslims in their criticisms of the doctrine of the Trinity have appeared to think that Christians believe in more than one God, which, of course, is untrue

Creator of the World

For both Muslims and Christians, God is the Creator of the world. Unlike the Bible, the Qur'an has only brief references to the creation of the world - the longest being Sura 41, 9-12:

Say: Is it that ye
Deny Him Who created
The earth in two Days?
And do ye join equals
With Him? He is
The Lord of (all) the Worlds.
He set on the (earth)
Mountains standing firm,
High above it,
And bestowed blessings on
The earth, and measured therein
Its sustenance
In four Days,
Alike for
(All) who ask.

Then He turned to the sky
And it had been (as) smoke:
He said to it
And to the earth:
"Come ye together,
Willingly or unwillingly ."
They said: "We do come
(Together), in willing obedience."

So He completed them
As seven firmaments
In two Days and He
Assigned to each heaven
Its duty and command.'

Perhaps because it is less interested than the Bible in how the world was created, the Qur'an speaks more about God's continuing work of creation. A commentary on Sura 7, 54, says , 'lest we should be obsessed with the Jewish idea that Allah *rested* on the seventh day, we are told that the Creation was but a prelude to Allah's work: for his authority is exercised constantly by the laws which He establishes and enforces in all parts of His creation.' The Arabic word for creation, *khalaqa* is used in the Qur'an of contemporary happenings. When the four stages of the embryo in the womb are described, it is said that God 'created' or 'made' each out of the previous one (23, 12-14):

Man we did create
From a quintessence (of clay)
Then we placed him
As (a drop of) sperm
In a place of rest,
Firmly fixed;
Then we made the sperm
Into a clot of congealed blood;
Then of that clot We made
A (foetus) lump; then We
Made out of that lump
Bones and clothed the bones
With flesh; then We developed
out of it another creature.
So blessed be Allah,
the Best to create.'

Lord of History

God is also Lord of history. Both the Bible and the Qur'an are 'sacral history', that is to say they describe past events as evidence of God's controlling activity. The Qur'an is less interested in chronology than the Old Testament, so that its references to past events are in no particular order. They are used as examples for the present. God exercises his control by sending 'natural' disasters as a punishment. For example the Flood, because of their wickedness, destroyed everyone except Noah and his family. Again, the destruction of Sodom and Gomorrah was a result of the evil behaviour of their inhabitants. God also initiates a series of events by 'calling' individuals, such as Abraham or Moses, to undertake a special task. God may also strengthen men to fight in battle and to gain victory.

Muslims tend to be more conscious of God's controlling influence on the course of events. The phrase '*insh'Allah* - 'if God wills it' is common, just as some Christians often used to say '*Deus vult'* (d.v.) Yet this does not mean that human behaviour is pre-determined, although at one time there were heated debates on the subject. The orthodox view is that all possibilities are created by God, but that human beings have the responsibility to 'acquire' actions out of the possibilities, thereby becoming accountable. Disobedience to God's will is, therefore, a human choice for which human beings are held responsible. The believer, however, is conscious that he or she only does the will of God through God's grace.

Mercy an d Judgment

The Qur'an begins 'In the Name of Allah, most gracious (*rahman*), most merciful (*rahim)*.' This description is often repeated and God's mercy is emphasised. There are said to be ninety-nine beautiful names of God. Many of them are to be found in the Qur'an. The names are recited on the Muslim rosary and according to a *hadith* or saying of the Prophet, anyone who repeats the names of God will be sure of Paradise.

Yet although Muslims speak so much of the Mercy and Compassion of God, Montgomery Watt, a Christian scholar with a deep knowledge of and sympathy for Islam, says in his *Islam and Christianity Today* that 'many Christians would claim that God as conceived by Christians is *more* loving that God as conceived by Muslims.' Yet, during the Middle Ages, Christendom was dominated by pictures and carvings of the Last Judgement. Traditionally Christians have spoken as if heaven was reserved for Christians and that others would go to hell. Montgomery Watt suggests that for Christians God is not only benevolent towards those who obey and love him, but God is like a shepherd who goes out to look for and rescue sheep that have gone astray. Perhaps the Christian emphasis on God rescuing the sinner relates to their teaching on original sin. Muslims reject this doctrine and believe that the individual is able to obey God's commands. Moreover, as Montgomery Watt notes, in the Qur'an, God loves all humanity and has sent to each community a prophet-messenger calling on them to serve God - so all people are given an opportunity of attaining 'the great success', which is life in Paradise.

There are passages in the Qur'an which suggest that those who fall away will not be given another chance, but the Epistle to the Hebrews also warns that

> 'It is impossible for those who have once been enlightened who have tasted the heavenly gift, who have shared in the Holy Spirit, who have tasted the word of God and the powers of the coming age, if they fall away, to be brought back to

repentance, because to their loss they are crucifying the Son of God all over again and subjecting him to public disgrace' (Hebrews 6, 4-6).

In Islam, the possibility of intercession on the Last Day was developed and with it the belief that Muhammad would intercede for the sinners of his community.

Montgomery Watt also suggests that 'beliefs about God's love 'are probably reflected in the treatment of sinners and criminals.' Farid Esack, a radical Muslim scholar from South Africa, however, comments in his *One Being a Muslim* that

'much of the talk of a "God of love" has become little more than Western conservative Christianity avoiding fundamental issues of structural social injustice and poverty in a society that prevents the love of Allah from being experienced in concrete terms in the daily lives of ordinary people. In condoning social suffering, [Christians] certainly have a lot of fellow travellers among some Muslim groups.'

Yet, in recent years, the World Council of Churches has proclaimed that God is on the side of the poor and its Anti-Racism programme was vocal in campaigning against structural oppression and racism. Moreover, even if for Christians the love of God is at the heart of the Gospel, the Bible also has stern warnings against injustice

Farid Esack is right that we need to walk a path between 'the apolitical fuzzy love of God and the relentless coldness of a distant Transcendent Being who only cares via retribution.' Perhaps this is one example of where Christians and Muslims need each other to find a proper balance and both to come closer to God's will.

The sort of comparison made by Montgomery Watt is unhelpful. There are so many variations in the attitudes and behaviour amongst people in different parts of the world and in different centuries who belong to the same religion that it is almost impossible to compare like to like. This is why the key question, as already suggested, is 'what is true religion?' What teachings and practices best promote that fullness of life that is God's will for human beings? Christians and Muslims are both called to be vigilant in ensuring that their communities live up to the highest ideals of their faith and maybe they can spur each other to good deeds. I have found that conversations with Muslim friends nearly always serve as a balancing corrective to my own views.

The way in which members of each faith can help members of the other find a truer balance also takes us back to the starting point of this chapter. I began with the sense of the holiness and majesty of God that I feel in some of the great mosques. The Bible too affirms God's holiness and at the communion service, Christians are invited to echo the angels' great hymn of praise:

'Holy, holy, holy, Lord,
God of power and might,
Heaven and earth are full of your glory.
Hosanna in the highest.

Yet perhaps some Christian worship today with its emphasis on fellowship and popular music has lost a sense of awe and holiness.

Christians believe that the glory of God is to be seen in the face of Jesus Christ. He awakes similar feelings of awe and fascination. Yet I wonder whether Christian worship at times in emphasising the love of God and Jesus' closeness to his followers may lose something of the sense of divine holiness. It is a question of balance. There are different emphases within religions, but perhaps Islam and Christianity can serve as correctives to each other. Both speak of a God who is transcendent. Isaiah speaks of God as 'the high and lofty One ... who lives forever, whose name is holy' (57, 15) and Sura 7. 54 says that God 'settled Himself on the Throne.' Yet the same verse of Isaiah has God say, 'I live in a high and holy place, but also with him who is contrite and lowly in spirit to revive the spirit of the lowly and to revive the heart of the contrite.' Islam also speaks of God who is close to the believer. In the Qur'an God says

'We know
What suggestions his soul
Makes to him: for We
Are nearer to him
Than (his) jugular vein.' (50, 16).

There is also a profound sense of God's intimacy and passionate love in the Sufi tradition. Sufis, like other mystics, long to experience the presence of God. They see life as a journey towards unity with God - a journey that involves death to the self, as this poem teasingly explains:

Before, as was my habit, self I claimed:
True Self I did not see, although I heard it named.
Being self-confined, true Self I did not merit,
Until, leaving self behind, I did Self inherit.

Sufism has given particular attention to the various stages of the spiritual journey One of the earliest and best accounts is the *Forty Station* (translated in Seyyed Hossein Nasr's *Living Sufism*) by the eleventh-century Sufi master Abu Sai'id ibn Abi'l Khayar. The thirty-ninth station is the supreme goal, to see God with they eye of the heart. The fortieth station purifies the Sufi from all desire.

Where there is a real attempt to listen to the other, even the doctrine of the Trinity may not be as divisive as it appears. The Qur'an insists on the Oneness of God. It classes amongst unbelievers those who say 'Allah is one of three' (5, 73), but that has never been orthodox Christian belief. It may be that some heretical Christians at the time of Muhammed were teaching this. The doctrine of the Trinity speaks of 'one substance and three persons', but the modern English use of the word 'person' is likely to distort the meaning of this formula. The original Greek word, *hypostasis*, was translated into Latin as *persona*, which meant an 'actor's mask' or a role in a play. It did not have the meaning of the modern English word person which suggests an independent self-conscious being. If the word person is taken in that sense, the doctrine of the Trinity can come near to tritheism.

In my understanding, belief in the Trinity affirms the Christian experience that God is known as our Creator and Sustainer, that God is also known in the life, teaching, death and resurrection of Jesus and that in both the fellowship of believers and in personal devotion God is present as the Holy Spirit. Further this speaks of Love - expressed in the mutual relationship of Father and Son bound together by the Spirit - as the Ultimate dynamic reality. Yet, I hesitate to say that the doctrine of the Trinity describes God's inner being and life. It is at best a pointer to a Mystery that we cannot fully fathom.

Hatif Isfahani, an eighteenth-century Persian poet, even praised Christians for affirming the Divine Unity:

> In the church I said to a Christian charmer of hearts,
> 'O thou in whose net the heart is captive!
> O thou to the warp of whose girdle each hair-top of mine is separately attached,
> "How long wilt thou continue not to find the way to the Divine Unity?
> How long wilt thou impose on the One the shame of the Trinity?
> How can it be right to name the one True God, 'Father, Son
> and Holy Ghost'?"
> She parted her sweet lips and said to me,

While with sweet laughter she poured sugar from her lips:
"If thou art aware of the secret of the Divine Unity
Do not cast on us the stigma of infidelity.
In three mirrors the Eternal Beauty cast a ray
From His effulgent countenance.
Silk does not become three things
If Thou callest it *Parinyan, Harir* and *Parand*."
While we were thus speaking, this chant
Rose up beside us from the church bell:
"He is One and there is naught save He:
There is no God save Him alone."

Although Muslims say that God is one, some Muslim thinkers said that God had a multiplicity of attributes. These were chiefly, omnipotence, omniscience, will, speech, hearing, seeing and life. The Ash'arites - followers of al-Ashari (873-935) a foremost Muslim theologian - held that the attributes 'were not God and not other than God.' Some Mediaeval Christian theologians who lived in the Muslim world and who wrote in Arabic compared the Christian hypostases with Islamic attributes. One writer said that the hypostases represented goodness, wisdom and power; another that they were existence, speech and life.

The intellectual problem is that if there is only One God and if this is over-emphasised, any separate identity of the created world is dissolved in Monism, so that despite appearances the natural world and human beings are part of God and have no independent being. These almost insoluble questions are those with which the Church fathers and mediaeval Muslim theologians wrestled. Some modern Christian thinkers, such as John Hick or Raimundo Panikkar, in their interpretation of the Trinity as a metaphor come close to Muslim thinking, but as the distinguished Muslim scholar Professor S A Ali observes, Muslims will always be uneasy with the language of 'Father, Son and Holy Spirit.'

This may all seem a little remote. It serves, however, to illustrate my major point that when you ask the meaning of a doctrine or, in other words, what was the insight or truth of experience that those who formulated these doctrines wanted to safeguard, you find yourself grappling, with them, with concepts almost too difficult for words. You find also that others using quite different terminology may be struggling with similar issues. As some Muslim and Christian thinkers come close enough to each other to understand the truths of experience which are enshrined in long-held doctrines, they find themselves speaking of same mysteries. They have moved beyond religious frontiers to the frontier which no thinker, however, brilliant can ever cross - to the meeting place of the human with the Divine where we find ourselves like Job speaking of things we do not understand, of 'things too wonderful for us to know' and where, in God's mercy, we may experience the reality of the One God whose glory passes our understanding. (Job, 42, - 6)

Chapter 3. THE HOLY QUR'AN.

Should the chapter on the Qur'an or on Muhammad come first? I have put the Qur'an first as it is for Muslims the Word of God and Muhammad's importance lies primarily in his role as messenger.

Recite

One day, when Muhammad was worshipping in the cave to which he was in the custom of retiring, he sensed a presence with him. It said to him, 'Recite' but he replied,'I am not able to recite.' The presence then seized him and clasped him to his bosom and again said,'Recite.' This happened three times, then, the presence released Muhammad telling him:

Proclaim! (or Recite)
In the name
Of thy Lord and Cherisher,
Who created -
Created man, out of
A leech-like clot:
Proclaim! And thy Lord
Is Most Bountiful, -
He who taught
(The use of) the Pen, -
Taught man that
Which he knew not. (96: 1-5).

When Muslims affirm that Muhammad is God's Prophet, this is the same as saying that his revelations really are from God - his message is the authentic voice of God. This is why also Muslims object to being called 'Mohammedans' - a term which used to be quite common.

For Muslims, the Qur'an is ultimate truth. Even to look on the Scripture with the reverence of a true believer constitutes, for devout Muslims, an act of worship to God. The Qur'an is God's speech, an eternal attribute existing within God's essence and sharing God's uncreatedness. Muslims handle the Holy Book with reverence and should perform ablutions, (*wudu'*) so as to be in a state of ritual purity before reading the scripture. The importance of calligraphy in the Muslim world also reflects the high dignity of the Qur'an. Not only in texts but also on buildings the elaboration of the visible word became a major art form, especially as representation of the human figure was not allowed lest it led to idolatry.

Only the Arabic text is in the proper sense the Qur'an. This is a major reason why most Muslims, wherever they live, learn Arabic, as I was reminded when I visited the remote Muslim community at the end of the old Silk Route in Xi'an in China This also helps to maintain the unity of the *umma* - or community - of all Muslims. The Qur'an has been translated into numerous languages, and at the Hamdard University in New Delhi, I was shown some of the early translations into Indian languages. Translations are, in effect, only commentaries.

The sounds of the Arabic, according to Al -Ghazali(d. 1111), perhaps the greatest teacher of Islam said, 'have become like the body and the dwelling-place for the divine wisdom and divine wisdom has become like the soul and spirit of the sounds.' Neal Robinson in *Discovering the Qur'an*, tries to illustrate this for English-speaking readers by comparing his translation of Muhammad's initial revelation (96, 1-4) with a transliteration of the Arabic. His English version is:

Read in the name of thy Lord who created.
He created man from a blood clot.
Read; and thy Lord is the most generous,
He who has taught with the pen
Taught man what he did not know.

The transliteration is:
iqra' bismi rabbi-ka 'l-ladhi khalaq
khalaqa 'l-insana min 'alaq
iqra' wa-rabbu-ka 'l-akram
al-ladhi 'allama bi-'l'qalam
'allama 'l-insana ma lam ya'lam.

It is at once clear that the original is characterised by rhyme and the whole Qur'an is either rhymed or assonance prose. The subdivisions of the *Suras* or chapters into *ayahs* or verses are on the basis of assonance. Although the verses are of unequal length, there is a marked rhythm.

The Qur'an is intended to be recited and during Ramadan, the month of fasting, Muslims go in large numbers to a mosque to hear extensive recitations of the Qur'an. In the course of a month, they would hear the whole Qur'an. There are usually recitations from the Qur'an also before or after the Friday congregational prayers. Muslims are encouraged to memorise the text, although some effort is required to learn to pronounce it correctly.

20

The Qur'an and the Bible are very different in composition. The messages of God, usually revealed by the angel Gabriel to Muhammad (2, 97), were received during a period of twenty three years and recorded in writing by pious scribes (80, 11-16). Already by the time of the Prophet's death, much of the Qur'an was written down and a large part of it was also known by heart. Just before the Prophet's death, he received confirmation that the revelation was complete:

This day have I
Perfected your religion
For you, completed
My favour upon you,
And have chosen for you
Islam as your religion (5, 3)

Muhammad needed no successor as a prophet. After his death the writings which recorded his messages, were gathered into a single book, according to the order that was established during the last Ramadan before Muhammad's death.

The Qur'an consists of 114 chapters *(Suras)*, composed of a varying number of verses *(ayahs)*. The chapters are not arranged chronologically, but in decreasing order of length - except for the first *Sura*, known as the Fatiha, which has only seven verses. The second *Sura* has 286 verses, whereas *Sura* 114 has only five verses. In general, the *Suras* which Muhammad received in the first part of his career come towards the end of the Qur'an.

Within thirteen years of his death, a number of complete copies were made by trusted Companions of the Prophet, working under the orders of Caliph Uthman. Copies were sent out in four directions, with a master copy retained at Madina. The occasional textual variants are explained by the *Hadith* or tradition that the Qur'an was revealed according to seven readings *(ahruf)*. The variants do not significantly affect the sense of the revelation. In modern editions, some orthographical marks have been added to help those who read the text aloud.

The Bible: A Library of Books

The Bible, by contrast, is a library of books of varying character. Simon Sebag Montefiore in *Jerusalem; The Biography* says, 'This sacred work of so many epochs and so many hands contains some facts of provable history, some stories of unprovable myth, some poetry of soaring beauty, and many passages of unintelligible, perhaps coded, perhaps simply mistranslated mystery. Most of it is written not to recount events but to promote a higher truth – the relationship of one people and their God. To the believer, the Bible is simply the fruit of divine revelation. To the historian, this is a contradictory, unreliable, repetitive source, often the only one available to us – and it is also, effectively, the first and paramount biography of Jerusalem.'

In the Hebrew Bible, there are historical books, books of prophecy and wisdom writings. The New Testament includes gospels, letters and a history of the early church as well as the book of Revelation. The Bible tells of events over a time span of some two thousand years. Most Biblical scholars agree that some of the books were written many years after the events to which they refer, although they incorporate earlier sources. Even the gospels were probably not written until some thirty to fifty years after the death of Jesus, although the material which they include circulated in oral form in the early Christian community.

When Muslims say that the Qur'an is the Word of God, they mean this in a more immediate sense than most Christians do when they say the Bible is the Word of God. The Qur'an speaks today. For the faithful reader, it is Remembrance (*dhikr),* it is Guidance (*huda*), it is Hearing (*shifa*), it is Mercy (*rahmah*), it is Blessed (*mubarak*), and it is always Most Generous (*karim*). It is the ultimate means of discrimination between right and wrong.

Christians also believe the Bible speaks today. Often after reading a passage in church, the reader will say 'This is the word of the Lord.' Yet in contemporary Christian thought Christ is the Word of God in the primary sense. The New Testament points beyond itself to that Word and is only the word of God in a secondary sense. As Kenneth Cragg, an Anglican scholar who has spent a lifetime in the study of Islam, wrote, 'The heart of the Christian revelation is the "event" of Jesus as the Christ, acknowledged as the disclosure in human form of the very nature of God. Hence the New Testament is a derivative from the prior and primary revelation of the living Word "made flesh and dwelling among us."'

Yet until the middle of the nineteenth century the majority of Christians would have regarded the Bible in much the same way as Muslims regard the Qur'an. The nineteenth century saw heated debates, in response to Darwin's theory of evolution and the beginnings of historical criticism of the Bible, as to whether the scripture was verbally inerrant. The general view now would be that the Holy Spirit inspired the human authors of Scripture, but did not dictate what they wrote.

With the development of the study of religions in the early twentieth century, many Western scholars applied the historical-critical methods used in the study of the Bible in their approach to the Qur'an. They studied and treated it not as scripture, but as any other book. Wilfred Cantwell Smith, a distinguished scholar in the study of religions, observed.

> 'Western students of the Qur'an tended to be either Christian or Jewish on the one hand, or secularist, perhaps atheist, on the other.' Accordingly, in both cases, they held that the 'Muslim view of the matter - the transcendentalist view, one might call it - was manifestly silly or perverse, and anyway was wrong; and therefore must be discounted.'

Western scholars pictured Muhammad writing the Qur'an - perhaps under divine inspiration - as an author might write any other book. Montgomery Watt, for example, suggested that 'the Qur'an is a collection of the messages that came to Muhammad from his unconscious (in a Jungian sense)' But scholarly discussion of how much Muhammad knew about Christianity and Judaism and of other influences upon him is for Muslims wide of the mark. For them, the Qur'an is a message that comes directly from God and was recited by Muhammad. Fazlur Rahman, who is sometimes labelled a Muslim modernist, insists that "he Muslim modernists say exactly the same thing as the so-called Muslim fundamentalists say: that Muslims must go back to the original and definitive sources of Islam and perform *ijithad* (independent judgment) on that basis.'

Fundamentalist

Yet because Muslims regard the Qur'an as literally the word of God, it is a mistake to regard them as 'fundamentalists' in the popular pejorative sense. The term 'Fundamentalist' was first used of some conservative Protestants in the USA who at the Niagara Conference of 1895 affirmed that certain beliefs were fundamental to Christianity and therefore non-negotiable. These beliefs, in reaction to evolutionary theories and Biblical criticism, included the verbal inerrancy of scripture, the virgin birth, a substitutionary theory of the atonement and the physical resurrection of Jesus Christ.

Recent studies have suggested that fundamentalism is a conscious reaction to and rejection of modern ways of thinking. It is useful to distinguish fundamentalists from those who are those who have not had cause to question traditional beliefs. As the distinguished scholar Seyyed Hossein Nasr wrote, 'For traditional man, Muslim or otherwise, that is a man whose life and thought are moulded by a set of principles of transcendent origin and who lives in a society in which these principles are manifested in every sphere' does not have cause to question the teaching of his religion. Fundamentalists are aware of the questioning and vigorously oppose it.

Fundamentalists reject the view that all knowledge is historically conditioned and hold that certain truths are true in an absolute and timeless sense. They also take a particular myth or symbol as true in the absolute sense. But in popular parlance, the term 'fundamentalist' denotes a person who has a closed mind and is often used with the word extremist to describe Muslims who are strongly opposed to Western society and its values. There is a small minority of Muslims to whom this description applies, but to assume that all Muslims because they believe the Qur'an to be literally the Word of God are ''fundamentalist' is a serious mistake.

Interpreting the Qur'an

Many Muslims who accept the absolute authority of the Qur'an, also engage in lively debate about its meaning and application in the contemporary world. The distinguished scholar Dr Irfan Ahmad Khan begins the Preface to his *Insight Into the Qur'an*, with the words, 'This book is an effort to understand the Qur'an with a modern mind.' While a text may be unchanging, its interpretation and application are made in a world which is ever changing. Islamic doctrine, law and thinking in general is based on four sources or fundamental principles. They are the Qur'an, the Traditions or *Sunna*, the Consensus of the Community (*ijma)* and individual thought (*ijtihad*).

Sunna is customary practice which primarily refers to the way in which the Prophet and his Companions lived and to what they said and did - as well as noticing those matters on which they were silent.It has been said that ''the *Sunna* forms the first living commentary on what the Qur'an means and thus becomes equally the foundation for Muslim life.' The concrete example of how the Prophet behaved sets the standard for the Muslim. His human acts and words were repeated as an example to the faithful. Many stories were told about him and a way had to be established of determining their authenticity. The *Sunna* of the Prophet was handed down in the form of short narratives told by one of the Companions or contemporaries. For example, Uqba ibn Amir said that 'someone sent the Prophet a

24

silk gown and he wore it during prayers, but on withdrawing he pulled it off violently with a gesture of disgust and said, "This is unfitting for a God-fearing man"'. Such a narrative is called a *hadith* or 'narrative.'

The way of checking authenticity was to establish the source of the tradition. If it was not told by one of the companions, then it was necessary to state the chain of authority going back to the original source of the narrative. By this means, *hadith* were classified as sound, good or weak. Various collections of *hadith* were made - primarily as legal precedents - and six collections were accepted as especially authoritative. For example, the collection (*Sahih*) made by al-Bukhari (810-70), who began the study of *hadith* at the age of 10 and who had a fine memory, contains over 7,000 narratives. al-Bukhari is said to have travelled widely and to have interviewed a thousand sheikhs, or religious leaders, and to have examined more than 200,000 *hadith*, rejecting many of them. His collection is divided into 97 'books' and sub-divided into 3,450 chapters. M M Khan's English translation runs to nine volumes. The collection by Muslim (817-75), who was born in Persia, who also travelled extensively, was made from 300,000 traditions and pays special attention to the chain of authorities. These two collections are amongst Islam's most holy books.

Ijma means the consensus of the community. It comes from a word meaning to gather or converge The word *jami'a*, which means the gathering of the faithful and is sometimes used of a mosque, comes from the same root. Only when the community of the faithful agrees is a principle or practice legitimated. *Ijma* has to be consistent with the Qur'an, the hadith and applied analogy (*qiyas*). According to Sunni tradition, the community of Muhammad would never agree on error. It is, therefore, the community of the faithful who are the guarantors of a true Islam. Authority rests with the community not with a 'Pope' or religious hierarchy. Islam has been a more democratic religion that Christianity. The Shi'a tradition, unlike, the Sunni does not accept *ijma*. Instead it relies on the light of the imams, whom Shi'ites believe receive special divine guidance and on the authority of ayatollahs - a modern title for religious leaders who gain a personal following. It is not surprising that the Shi'a community, which accepts charismatic leadership, is also more fragmented.

In the Sunni community it is a matter of debate whether the fourth source of authority, *ijthad,* which means independent judgement, based on study and acknowledged expertise, is still open. Rigorists claim that earlier *ijtihad* completed its task and a final *Shari'a* or code of legal practice is now in force. Others believe that reinterpretation of the law in changing circumstances may be possible. In Shi'a

Islam, the *mujtahid*, who makes and mediates such judgements, has an important role. In Sunni tradition, the emphasis is on the *Ulama* - those who are learned in Islamic law and teaching, whose task is to express the mind or consensus of the community. Many members of the *Ulama* are great scholars with a deep knowledge of Islamic scriptures and traditions.

An explanation of the sources of authority helps to explain how the Muslim world reacts to change and in part explains why there is much variety in Muslim practice and teaching. Some groups, as in every religion, of course, claim that their expression of the faith is the only true Islam. Another reason for variety is that there are several interpretations of the *Shari'a* or religious law, which gives a systematic description of how Muslims should live.

There are four classic schools. The Hanafites recognise that the Qur'an and the *hadith* do not decide every issue so there is place for properly informed opinion and judgement. The Malikites are more cautious about the use of hadith. The Shafi'ites and even more so, the Hanbalites, stress the control of the Qur'an and *hadith* alone. Thus different schools allow more or less freedom for informed opinion. The Hanafites attach more attention to the principle of the law than its letter. Thus if any law deduced by analogy is inequitable, harsh or inconvenient, then the Hanafite jurist is at liberty to discard it and to adopt one that is convenient and humane. This is not an arbitrary process but a method of using the principles of Law to fit the circumstances of a given case. Different traditions may, therefore, adopt different attitudes, for example, as to the use of contraceptives.
In some parts of the Muslim world the most conservative traditions have become dominant and have created in the West an unfairly rigorist view of Islam. The Wahhabiya movement, which has become dominant in Saudi Arabia, is based on the Hanbalite Sharia, which as we have seen gives hardly any lee-way for human opinion and judgement. Basing their teaching only on the Qur'an and the authentic Sunna, they reject 1,400 years of development in Islamic theology and mysticism. Punishments are rigorous and anything from non-Islamic sources is to be opposed. Hence those schooled in this tradition will be suspicious of Western cultural influence, especially when it is linked to military or economic oppression. There is therefore a profound struggle in the Muslim world for the soul of Islam. This is a subject to which we return.

Muslim and orthodox Jewish attitudes to scripture have made me look again at the assumptions of the historical-criticism of scripture in which I was trained. Essentially, the historical-critical approach tries to identify what a text meant to those for whom it was first written. This means trying to identify editorial work and the various sources which have been brought together to create the Biblical text as we now have it. This is a skilled and disciplined task and applies the methods of textual and historical scholarship to the Bible. It has greatly enriched our knowledge. Yet, as Cantwell Smith pointed out, this approach reflects the individualism of the West. 'Central or basic was deemed to be the meaning of the individual person who said or wrote something: his or her intention.' Linked to this is what Cantwell Smith calls the historical fallacy that the Qur'an is 'fundamentally or exclusively a seventh-century document', linked to the assumption that its author was Muhammad and not God. Scripture like any great piece of writing - and more so - has a life of its own. It does not have one fixed meaning but addresses each individual reader. There is a *hadith* which has God saying, 'when someone recites or reads the Qur'an, that person is, as it were, entering into conversation with Me and I into conversation with him or her.'

It is a common place to suggest that the Gospels as we now have them reflect the concerns of the Christian community in the second half of the first century - the period in which the Gospels were probably written. Much effort has gone into identifying what Jesus actually said or did. Some scholars say there is little that we can know with certainty, others are more confident. But this raises the question of where does scriptural authority lie. Is it with the text as we have received it or with the supposed reconstruction of the scholar? Some Christian scholars are now more interested in the text as we have it and in the history of how it has been used and understood over the centuries by the Church. Although scripture derives its authority from God, in a sense it is the community that regards a text as authoritative that bestows authority upon it. This means that past arguments amongst Christians about the rival authority of Church and Bible lose their importance. The two are inseparable. Similarly, the Muslim affirmation that Muhammad is the Prophet of God implies that the message he delivered is indeed from God.

Some understanding of the place of scripture in other faith communities can help Christians be more aware of their particular view of scripture. There is also great benefit in reading passages of scripture together with Jews and Muslims. They can bring new insights to familiar passages. Most important of all, the Qur'an, 'a mercy to the worlds' can be a book of inspiration to all who are believers in God. Arthur Arberry wrote that the task of translating the Quran, which he undertook, not lightly, and carried to its conclusion at a time of great personal distress ... comforted (him) in a manner for which he will always be grateful. He therefore acknowledges his gratitude to whatever power or Power inspired the man and the Prophet who first recited these scriptures.

Chapter 4. THE PROPHET MUHAMMAD

'I bear witness that there is no god but God and Muhammad is the messenger of God.' 'This Confession of Faith (*Shahada*) is the first 'Pillar of Islam.'

Muhammad through Christian eyes

'Does Muhammad also have a message for Christians?' was the question discussed at a conference that I arranged through the World Congress of Faiths. It was led by Bishop Kenneth Cragg, who had an expert and longtime personal knowledge of Islam.

Muslims, as we shall see in a later chapter, regard Jesus as a prophet and are often resentful that Christians do not reciprocate the compliment, although I am happy to speak of Muhammad as a prophet. Ulfat Aziz-us-Samd, in his *Comparative Study of Christianity and Islam* complained that:

> 'While Muslims believe in Jesus Christ as a true prophet and love and respect him ... Christians not only reject Muhammad, but are never tired of speaking about him and his religion in the most disparaging manner possible. They declare him to be a victim of hallucination, or even of epilepsy. They attribute unworthy motives to him and claim to find many faults in his character and in his private and public life.'

Early Christian accounts of Muhammad's life were usually derogatory. Christians in the past have spoken of Muhammad as a heretic, with a false or inadequate understanding of God. He was depicted as a war-like aggressor or as promiscuous because he had several wives, although some marriages were partly for diplomatic alliances. The great Christian poet Dante placed Muhammad in the inferno, torn to pieces by pigs. Luther regarded Muhammad and the Pope as the two arch-enemies of Christ. In the twentieth century, H G Wells said Muhammad was a man 'whose life on the whole was by modern standards unedifying.' Some recent comments in the media or the web have been far worse.

Some Christians, however, have written quite objective accounts of Muhammad's life and teaching. One of the first British writers to attempt a more sympathetic portrait was Thomas Carlyle (1795-1881), who saw Muhammad as a genuine hero among the prophets. F D Maurice (1805-72) in his lectures on Islam was not entirely unsympathetic. The twentieth century saw many more scholarly accounts of Muhammad's life and times, although the historical-critical presuppositions of some scholars were unacceptable to Muslims.

Few even of the best accounts of Muhammad's life discuss the religious significance of Muhammad for those who are Christian. The study of religions, which as an academic discipline developed quite quickly during the twentieth century, stressed the need for neutrality and impartiality. The phenomenological approach took seriously the faith of the believer and tried to appreciate a religion from the standpoint of its adherents. In arranging the World Congress of Faiths conference I felt that an interfaith group could perhaps go further and try to discuss the *religious* significance of one faith to members of another. The revelation of the Qur'an is in intention a universal message addressed to all people 'a mercy to the world' Can those who belong to another household of faith also hear in it a word of God?

A rather similar question is whether non-Muslims should speak about the 'Prophet' Muhammad. For me as a Christian, Muhammad is not *the* Prophet or the seal of the prophets. Yet, I believe that his was a genuine encounter with God and that his was a prophetic message, akin to that of the great Biblical prophets Isaiah and Jeremiah.

In this I agree with W Montgomery Watt who gave rather more extended arguments. He wrote:

'Muhammad claimed to receive messages from God and conveyed these to his contemporaries. On the basis of these messages a religious community developed, claiming to serve God, numbering some thousands in Muhammad's lifetime, and now having several hundred million members. The quality of life in the community has been on the whole satisfactory for the members. Many men and women in this community have attained to saintliness of life, and countless ordinary people have been enabled to live decent and moderately happy lives in difficult circumstances. These points lead to the conclusion that the view of reality presented in the Qur'an is true and from God, and that therefore Muhammad is a genuine prophet.'

Keith Ward, who was Regius Professor of Theology at Oxford, has written:

'Christians can see Muhammad as truly inspired by God, as called to proclaim a strict monotheistic faith, and as chosen by God for that purpose. In seeing him thus, they can place him on the same level as all the prophets of Israel and the apostles of the early Christian church. It may even be possible to place him, from an authentically Christian viewpoint, on the same level as Jesus, insofar as prophet-hood is concerned (remembering that, for Christians, Jesus is "more than a prophet". In other words, a Christian can see Muhammad as inspired in the same sense as Jewish and Christian prophets, and thus accord him the highest honour as a true prophet. Nevertheless, they would in this still fall short of the Muslim perception that Muhammad was uniquely chosen to utter the definitive and unquestionable words of God himself.'

So I use the title 'Prophet' of Muhammad partly as a sign of my reverence for him and partly out of respect for the religious convictions of those who are Muslim.

Underlying this approach is my conviction that there is One God who has spoken in various ways through the great religious traditions. While, in my view, there is a transcendent unity of faiths, there is also considerable difference and variety. In part this is because people's apprehension of and response to the divine is varied, especially because of cultural and historical differences, but also each tradition emphasises certain central truths. We need to listen to these and see how, if we belong to a different faith community, they illuminate or challenge the convictions that we already hold.

So the approach of the conference was to try to hear the message Muhammad recited and to listen in it for a word of God to those of another community of faith. His emphasis on the Oneness of God and the rejection of idolatry is perhaps a corrective to those forms of Christianity which so focus on Jesus as almost to forget the Father. Orthodox Christian worship is not primarily worship of Jesus but worship of God through Jesus Christ. Islam too, as I have suggested, can remind Christians of the glory and holiness of God.

The Life of Muhammad

There is now considerable scholarly agreement about the main events in Muhammad's life. He was born in 570 CE. at Mecca, which was a busy commercial centre in Arabia with a near monopoly of the entrepôt trade between the Indian ocean and the Mediterranean. Muhammad was of the family Banu

Hashim of the tribe of the Quraysh. He was born after the death of his father and became ward of his grandfather, Abd al-Muttalib. At an early age he had an experience of a visitation by two figures - later identified as angels - who 'opened his chest and stirred their hands inside' It was the first of several unusual experiences that led Muhammad increasingly to search on his own for the truth of God. This quest was strengthened when he was employed by a widow, called Khadijah, to take trading caravans north to Syria. There he met Christians and Jews, especially the monk Bahira who recognised in him the signs of the promised Messiah. By now Muhammad was under the protection of his uncle Abu Talib. At the age of 25, he married Khadijah. They had two sons who died young and four daughters. Muhammad was increasingly influenced by the Hanifs, who sought to preserve a monotheism which they traced back to Ibrahim (Abraham). The people of Mecca, however, were polytheistic and worshipped idols. Muhammad often went by himself to a cave on Mount Hira. It was there that as has been said, that he had the strong sense of a presence, later identified with Gabriel.

At first Muhammad thought he was possessed, but as he fled the cave and was half way down the mountain, he heard a voice saying to him, 'O Muhammad, thou art the messenger of God and I am Gabriel.' On his return home, with a still quaking heart, he said to Khadija 'Cover me, cover me.' Khadijah went to tell her cousin Waraqah, who was old and blind. Waraqh, who was a Christian, exclaimed that the angel of Revelation who had come to Moses had now come to Muhammad. A further divine revelation reassured Muhammad. After further revelations, he began preaching, but met strong opposition. He was clear that if God is God and God is One, then there cannot be a Christian God and a Jewish God and certainly not the many deities of Mecca. He was also convinced that the idolatry of Mecca had to be swept away. For Muhammad there was only One God from whom all creation derived. Therefore all human beings should live in a corresponding unity (*umma*). Islam is the attempt to realise this unity under God.

Abu Bakr, after his wife Khadijah, his cousin Ali and his slave Zayd - whom the Prophet set free - was the first of the believers. They were called *al-muslimun* or Muslims, those who enter into a condition of safety because of their commitment to God.

Opposition and persecution increased. But then, Muhammad was invited to Yathrib - soon to be known as Madina - to make his way of unity a practical reality by reconciling the town's two rival ruling families. He made this move, known as the *Hijra*, which means emigration and breaking the bonds of kinship, in 622, a date which was to become the first year of the Muslim calendar. There under the guidance of fresh revelations from God he began to establish a community. These revelations were clearly distinct from the words that Muhammad spoke as an ordinary human being. It is said that his appearance changed and the style of utterance, which was rhythmic and with a loose pattern of rhyme, was different to his normal speech.

At Madina, Muhammad was joined by some seventy other emigrants, known as the Muhajirun. Opposition from Mecca continued, partly because Muhammad raided some of their caravans. In 624 the Muslims defeated a much larger Meccan army at the battle of Badr, but in the following year the battle of Uhud, in which the Prophet was injured, was inconclusive. This was largely because the archers disobeyed their orders because they were too eager for booty. In 627 the Quraysh failed in their attempt to besiege Madina. Then in 630, Muhammad captured Mecca and purified it from idols. Besides these military engagements, Muhammad both organised the pattern of life in Madina and built up relations with neighbouring tribes.

Muhammad died two years after his return to Mecca. He had often spoken of Paradise and according to his wife A'ishah, his last words were, 'With the supreme communion in Paradise, with those upon whom God hath showered His favour, the prophets and the saints and the martyrs and the righteous, most excellent for communion are they.' (4, 69).

After the Prophet's death

Despite his various marriages, Muhammad had no surviving son. His nearest relation was his cousin Ali, who had married one of his daughters, but the majority of the community chose as his successor Abu Bakr, who was one of his first followers. There were those, however, who thought that Ali should have been his successor and within a generation of Muhammad's death, this lead to the division of Islam between Sunni and Shi'a, which persists to this day.

Almost immediately after Muhammad's death, Abu Bakr (d.634) declared, 'If any of you have been worshipping Muhammad, let him know that Muhammad is dead. But if you have been worshipping God, then know that God is eternal and never dies.'
   'Muhammad is no more than a Messenger:
   Many were the Messengers that passed away
   Before Him.' (3, 144).

Muhammad is not regarded as superhuman, nor divine, nor without sin. He was commanded in the Qur'an:

Say: "I am but a man
Like yourselves, (but)
The inspiration has come
To me, that your God is
One God." (18, 110).

Nonetheless Muhammad is special and is sometimes called *insan al-kamil*, the perfect man - much as Christians think of Jesus in his humanity as the perfect human being. He is regarded as the exemplar and first living commentary on the meaning of the Qur'an and how to apply it to daily life. He had a particular intensity of communion with God. Countless stories, *hadith* were told about him and his sayings and actions inform the mind of the Muslim

Constance Padwick who made a careful study of Muslim Prayer Manuals that were in common use, wrote:

'No one can estimate the power of Islam as a religion who does not take into account the love at the heart of it for this figure. It is here that human emotion, repressed at some points by the austerity of the doctrine of God as developed in theology, has its full outlet - a warm human emotion which the peasant can share with the mystic. The love of this figure is perhaps the strongest binding force in a religion which has so marked a binding power.'

The scholar and active inter-faith worker Irfan Ahmad Khan explains the 'unique status' of the Prophet.

'Being a human, the Prophet shares all those limitations which human beings necessarily have and from which God alone is free. However, in the following sense the Prophet is infallible. As the Prophet explains the Divine Book to his people and works for the fulfillment of its practical demands, God watches and whenever needed He intervenes (58, 1-4; 80, 1-10). Subsequently, what is conveyed to the people is free of any mistake.'

With the Prophet's death, revelation came to an end. No one inherited Muhammad's infallibility as the mouthpiece of God. Irfan Ahmad Khan makes entirely clear that 'it is a very serious mistake to consider the Qur'an which is revealed guidance in divine words as the Prophet's words.' Great attention is paid to the sayings of the Prophet but they do not have the same authority as the divinely revealed message of the Qur'an. It is interesting that St Paul in writing about marriage distinguishes between the command of the Lord and his own instruction. He writes to the Corinthians: 'To the married I give this command (not I, but the Lord)... To the rest I say this (I, not the Lord) (I Corinthians 7, 10 and 12). Later in the chapter Paul writes, 'Now about virgins: I have no command from the Lord, but I give a judgement as one who by the Lord's mercy is trustworthy.'

Great authority, therefore, attaches to the sayings of Muhammad, but as Dr Irfan Ahmad Khan makes clear, Muhammad's directions are not independent of the Book, but its interpretation and amplification. For example, whatever the Prophet says about Ramadan should be seen as explaining the Qur'anic instruction about it that 'whosoever observes the month, should fast during it.' (2, 183ff).

It is not, however, just a question of authority, but of deep devotion. Constance Padwick in her book *Muslim Devotion* quoted one of the prayers that a Muslim pilgrim might say standing before the Tomb of the Prophet at Madina: 'I bear witness that you are the apostle of God. You have conveyed the message. You have fulfilled the trust. You have counselled the community and enlightened the gloom and shed glory on the darkness, and uttered words of wisdom.'

Ezedine Guellouz's account of his pilgrimage to the Prophet's tomb is simpler, but just as moving. After praying in the Prophet's Garden, he writes:

'Then we resume our progress (from East to West) towards the room where the Prophet's tomb is. A simple greeting. "Peace be upon you, O Prophet, and the mercy and blessing of God!" Nothing more than one might say to a friend. One is advised not to raise one's voice, not to bow, not to make any gesture of greeting towards the screen, nor towards the grille, still less to kiss them, or to pray in their direction. All the religious books stress these points. On the other hand, there is no reason why one should not pray God to bless Muhammad and to reward him for all that he did in the service of God and for the salvation of Mankind. We can also convey to the Prophet the greetings of those who have asked us to do so...'

Every Muslim longs to hear, at death, the words:
(To the righteous soul will be said:)
"O (thou) soul,
In (complete) rest
And satisfaction!

34

Come back thou
To thy Lord -
Well pleased (thyself)
And well-pleasing
Unto Him!
Enter thou, then,
Among my Devotees!
Yea, enter thou
My Heaven. (89, 26-30).

Constance Padwick remarked that Islam has to be ever on its guard against what may be a tacit, though never explicit, deifying of the Prophet. Perhaps the devotion offered by some Christians to the Blessed Virgin Mary may be a parallel. The theological question about when veneration becomes worship need not detain us. The important point here is for Christians to be aware of the deep love that faithful Muslims have for the Prophet Muhammad, of whom they say, whenever they mention his name, 'Peace be upon him.' Christians need to learn more about Muhammad so as to dispel inherited and lingering prejudice.

Initially Muhammad put up with great courage with the abuse and persecution heaped upon him. Even when odiously reviled he did not answer back. Once when he was in prostration in the courtyard of the Ka'aba, someone placed the entrails of a camel over his shoulders, but he continued in his prayers until his daughter came and removed them so that he could get up. He remained constant in his faith during long years of frustration. Although regular prayer and an annual fast is required of Muslims, the Qur'an says:

So woe to the worshippers
Who are neglectful
Of their Prayers,
Those who (want but)
To be seen,
But refuse (to supply)
(Even) neighbourly needs' (107, 4-7).

Muhammad said, 'He who does not give up uttering falsehood and misconduct abstains in vain from food and drink during the fast, as Allah does not require merely physical compliance from him'.

Although the Prophet stressed the importance of fasting, he equally insisted on the need to break the fast. Islam is not an ascetic religion. Muhammad said to Uthman ibn Maz'un who was ascetic by nature and who asked permission to make himself a eunuch and to spend the rest of his life as a wandering beggar,

'Hast thou not in me a fair example? And I go into women, and I eat meat, and I fast, and I break my fast. He is not of my people who maketh men eunuchs or maketh himself a eunuch.'

Thinking that Uthman had not fully understood what he meant, he told him that he should not fast every day,

'For verily thine eyes have their rights over thee, and the body hath its rights, and thy family has rights. So pray, and sleep, and fast, and break fast.

The Qur'an stresses the importance of giving thanks to God for the gifts of life, for the rich provision of nature,(6, 98-99) for blessings of life, such as hearing and sight and sleep:

And among His Signs
Is the sleep that ye take
By night and by day.' (30, 23).

The Qur'an also speaks of the joy of marriage as a sign of God's mercy.

And among His Signs
Is this, that he created
For you mates from among
Yourselves, that ye may
Dwell in tranquillity with them,
And He has put love
And mercy between your (hearts):
Verily in that are Signs
For those who reflect. (30, 21)

Muhammad himself was a man of deep prayer and, besides the five required times of prayer, would spend much other time in prayer. He was also a person of great compassion. There are many stories of his kindness to animals. I like the one of the occasion when he came into a house and put down his cloak. Whilst he was talking, a mother cat and her kittens settled on the cloak. Rather than disturb the cats, Muhammad took a knife and cut round them leaving the cats part of his cloak.

His compassion was shown too in his treatment of his enemies. After the capture of Mecca, Muhammad sent for the leaders of the Quraish. They appealed for mercy and the Holy Prophet responded in words similar to those used by Joseph to his brothers:

'This day
Let no reproach be (cast)
On you: Allah will forgive you,
And He is the Most Merciful.'
Of those who show mercy!' (12, 92).

Despite all the scorn and hatred, the hardship and suffering, in the moment of victory Muhammad granted a general amnesty and chose the way of reconciliation. The Prophet showed great skill in diplomacy and his truthfulness was recognised.

Muhammad united in himself love for God and love for other people, as this prayer shows
O Lord, grant us to love You;
Grant that we may love those that love You;
Grant that we may do the deeds that win Your love.
Make the love of You to be dearer to us than ourselves,
Than our families, than wealth, and even than cool water.

W. Montgomery Watt spoke of Muhammad's three great gifts: first, his gift as a seer or prophet; secondly, his wisdom as a statesman and thirdly his skill and tact as an administrator. The more I read of his life, the more my respect for Muhammad grows.

When Aishah, his favourite wife, was asked what sort of character the Prophet possessed, she answered, 'Have you not read the Qur'an?...Truly the character of the Prophet was the Qur'an.'

Chapter 5. ISLAM AND CHRISTIANITY

The Gospel According to Islam is an attractive little book that I was given some time ago. In it, Ahmad Shafaat presents the material about Isa (Jesus) which is to be found in the Qur'an in the style of one of the Synoptic Gospels. He supplements this with material from the Gospels, but only where such material fits the basic Islamic presuppositions about Jesus. Thus, the purification of Jesus, as told by St Luke is included, but not the birth narratives, because there is already a rather different account of his birth in the Qur'an. Several of Jesus' sayings are included, but no mention of the claim that he was Son of God.

The presuppositions of the *Gospel According to Islam* reflect Islam's attitude to Judaism and Christianity. It is accepted that both religions are 'Religions of the Book', but that where they differ from the teaching of Qur'an this is because Jews and Christians have corrupted the original message of their prophets. The claim is that Islam is the one true religion - the eternal message of God to humanity, which has been declared by all past prophets, but which is now proclaimed again in its final and incorruptible form in the Qur'an. The claim is strikingly similar to that made for Jesus Christ at the beginning of the Epistle to the Hebrews - a passage often read at the Christmas communion service.

'When in former times God spoke to our forefathers, he spoke in fragmentary and varied fashion through the prophets. But in this final age he has spoken to us in the Son whom he has made heir to the whole universe, and through whom he created all orders of existence: the Son who is the effulgence of God's splendour and the stamp of God's very being, and sustains the universe by the word of power.' (Hebrews 1, 1-3)

It is understandable that believers will claim that theirs is the final truth. Absolute truth is often thought to be the concomitant of the total dedication that faith requires. There are those, however, today, with whom I sympathise, who question the possibility of absolute truth and who adopt a 'pluralist' position which accepts that different faiths have particular insights into Truth, but that the Ultimate Divine Mystery is beyond full comprehension by the human mind.

Indeed, long ago the Sufis, as we shall see, pointed to this transcendent unity of religion. Dr Seyyed Hossein Nasr in *Living Sufism* explains that the Sufi

'is one who seeks to transcend the world of forms, to journey from multiplicity to Unity, from the particular to the Universal. He leaves the many for the One and through this very process is granted the vision of the One in the many. For him all forms become transparent, including religious forms... Sufism or Islamic gnosis is the most universal affirmation of that perennial wisdom which stands at the heart of Islam and in fact of all religion as such. It is this supreme doctrine of Unity... that the Sufis call the "the religion of love." This love is not merely sentiment or emotion, it is the realised aspect of gnosis. It is a transcendental knowledge that reveals the inner unity of religions.'

The majority of Christians have claimed an absolute truth for their religion - even for their branch of that religion. They should, therefore, be able to understand the traditional Muslim position. The question, however, we shall have to consider is whether this means that there will inevitably be a clash between followers of these two great religions.

It is possible to make the claim for final truth in an absolutist manner. For example, the Catholic Council of Florence in 1438-45 declared that 'no one remaining outside the Catholic Church, not just pagans, but also Jews or heretics or schismatics, can become partakers of eternal life, but they will go to the "everlasting fire which was prepared for the devil and his angels", unless before the end of life they are joined to the Church.' A somewhat similar attitude is shown by the, perhaps apocryphal, reply of the second Caliph, Umar, to a question, after the Egyptian city of Alexandria was captured, about what to do with the great library there. He is reported to have replied, 'If the books are in agreement with the Qur'an, they are unnecessary and may be destroyed; if they are not in agreement with the Qur'an, they are dangerous and should certainly be destroyed.' In fairness to Caliph Umar it should be added that he permitted Jewish families to resettle in Jerusalem, despite protests from some Christians, and that he personally supervised the cleansing of the Temple Mount.

A more eirenic approach acknowledges that there is truth in other traditions, although the final truth is that of the tradition to which the believer himself belongs. Paul said that 'God hath not left himself without witness' (Acts 14, 17). Liberal Christians today would adopt an 'inclusivist' position which recognises that God is revealed in all the great religions, but that God's final definitive revelation is in Jesus Christ. In a similar way, many Muslims recognise the God's has declared his will in past generations, but that the authoritative message is that given to the Prophet Muhammad. According to one of the Prophet's sayings, every human being is a muslim, in the sense that his or her true purpose is to serve God. 'Every child is born in the *fitrah* (the natural state) and it is his parents who make him into a Jew or a Christian. Just as a camel is born whole - do you perceive any defect?' In this context the word parents has the wider meaning of social influences or social environment. So, in the words of Ismail al-Faruqi, 'the historical religions are out growths of *din al-fitrah*, containing within them differing amounts or degrees of it.'

The Qur'an states that

We assuredly sent
Amongst every People a Messenger,
(With the Command), "Serve
Allah, and eschew Evil" (16,36).

It says also that 'For every nation there is a messenger.' Traditionally the number of prophets is said to be 124,000. Again it is stated, 'Nothing is said to thee that was not said to the messengers before thee' (41, 43). Mention is made of Noah and Abraham and Moses and Jesus and other prophets (6, 84-86),

Since only some of God's apostles are mentioned in the Qur'an (40, 78), the Buddha and the avatars of the Hindus are not necessarily excluded. Certainly the Qur'an denounces idolatry and Muslims when they reached India attacked idolatry verbally and then physically. But it is now recognised by some Muslim scholars that, like early Christian missionaries, the first Muslims did not understand role of 'idols' or 'images' in Hinduism. I once heard a lecture at a conference in Delhi by the African Muslim scholar Professor Dawud O S Noibi who said that the phrase 'People of the Book' is better translated as 'followers of earlier revelations.' He stressed that the Qur'an teaches that God has sent every people a prophet and he suggested that Rama, Krishna and Zoroaster might be seen as prophets of Allah. Later on the same day that I had heard the lecture, I visited the great Jama Masjid in Old Delhi. The guide mentioned that Islam teaches that every people has been sent a prophet, such as Moses or Jesus or Krishna or Rama or Zoroaster. Perhaps the Professor from Africa was only acknowledging what many Muslims who have lived for centuries in a religiously plural society have known for a long time.

Isa in the Qur'an

The Qur'an makes a number of references to Isa (Jesus) and also refers to John the Baptist and Mary. Geoffrey Parrinder in his *Jesus and the* Qur'an, was right when he said that 'the Qur'an gives a greater number of honourable titles to Jesus than to any other figure of the past.' Jesus is mentioned in 93 verses, although Job is mentioned more often. Ibrahim (Abraham) and Musa (Moses) are also given great importance. Jesus is always regarded with reverence by Muslims, who add, 'May God bless him', whenever they mention his name. As Seyyed Hossein Nasr says:

'For the Muslim, within the firmament of Islam, in which the Prophet is like the full moon, the other great prophets and saints are like stars which shine in the same firmament, but they do so by the grace of Muhammad - upon whom be peace. A Muslim can pray to Abraham or Christ, not as Jewish or Christian prophets, but as Muslim ones, and in fact often does so, as seen in the popular "prayer of Abraham" in the Sunni world and the *Du'a-yi warith* in Shi'ite Islam.'

This respect for those of other faiths was shown by the Prophet himself who when a delegation of sixty Orthodox Christians of Najran came to make a pact with the Prophet, were received by Muhammad in the Mosque. He allowed the Christians to pray there, which they did facing East. It is on this occasion that the revelation was received which says:
'The similitude of Jesus
Before Allah is as that of Adam.' (3, 59).

The Qur'an speaks of the Virgin birth and of Jesus' miracles and teaching. There is also an appeal by God that Christians should return to the proper path of faith and cease to exaggerate the status of Jesus. But, as I said at the beginning, where the Qur'an and the Bible disagree, the Bible has to be wrong, because the Qur'an is God's final revelation. As Imam Abduljalil Sajid says, 'For us Muslims, the only true version can be the Qur'anic account.' He speaks, however, of the confusion caused for young Muslims by school celebrations of the nativity. He recounts that a few years ago a teacher in a Madrasa (religious school) asked his students whether they thought that Jesus was the Son of God. Most of the children in the class put up their hands to indicate that they thought he was.

Did God have a Son?

The Qur'an accepts the 'Virgin Birth' of Jesus. It is easy for God to do this as God can accomplish his purposes in the way he wishes (19, 21; 45, 7). But it is made clear that Jesus is the son of Mary, a sign to men and a mercy from God, but not the 'Son of God.'

'It is not be fitting
To (the majesty) of Allah
That He should beget

A son. Glory be to Him!
When he determines
A matter, He only says
To it, "Be" and it is. (19, 35).

The Qur'an always refers to Jesus in respectful terms. He is called a "sign", a "mercy", a "witness" and an "example". He is called by his proper name and by the titles Messiah and Son of Mary and by the names Messenger, Prophet, Servant, Word and Spirit of God. The Qur'an, however, as we have seen, denies the doctrine of the Trinity and rejects the belief that God had a Son. There are many Qur'anic denunciations of the idea that God has male or female offspring or has acquired a son, but at least some of these should probably be taken as referring to pagan gods and goddesses. There are three clear denials of Jesus' divinity.

'Say, "He is Allah,
The One;
Allah, the Eternal; Absolute;
He begetteth not,
Nor is He begotten;
And there is none
Like unto Him"' (Sura 112).

O People of the Book!
Commit no excesses
In your religion: nor say
Of Allah aught but the truth.
Christ Jesus the son of Mary
Was (no more than)
A Messenger of Allah .
Say not "Three": Desist:
It will be better for you:
For Allah is One God:
Glory be to Him:
(Far exalted is He) above
having a son.' (4, 171).

'The Jews say "Uzair [Ezra] is a son
Of Allah", and the Christians
Say "Christ is the Son of Allah"
That is a saying from their mouths;

(In this) they but imitate
What the Unbelievers of old
Used to say. Allah's curse
Be on them....
And (they take as their Lord)
Christ the son of Mary;
Yet they were commanded
To worship but One God:
There is no god but He.
Praise and glory to Him. (9, 30-31).

Muslims deny the divinity of Jesus because they reject all idea of God's physical paternity, which, of course, Christians also reject. They also think that the teaching of the incarnation threatens the unity of God, although the doctrine of the Trinity is intended by Christians to guard against this danger.

In part the disagreement is a matter of language and of a failure to go beyond what is said to what is meant. Many Christians react with defensiveness and even hostility if someone denies that Jesus is the Son of God. But perhaps Christians are not always aware that the language can be misleading. As the American Catholic theologian Monika Hellwig in *Jews and Christians Speak of Jesus* has said 'The serious and apparently intractable difficulties in Christology begin in a simplification in Gentile context and language of the elusive Hebrew way of speaking about the mystery of God and of God's dealings with creation and history.' In my book *Christian-Jewish Dialogue*, I suggested that the early Christians were cautious about speaking of Jesus as God and that 'it could be said of second-century Christology that Christ was still the incarnate Logos, God's revelation become flesh and blood. Christ was not yet the third person of the Trinity.' In time, the teaching that God is Three Persons in One God came to be understood in a way that increased the distance between Jews and Muslims, on the one hand, and Christians on the other. In the book, I also asked whether there is other language which will more effectively communicate what Christians really believe. 'To communicate the mystery of God's presence in Jesus Christ today may mean starting again, as the language of the creeds may be a hindrance rather than a help... It is the living experience of faith behind the formularies that we need to discover. True Christian continuity is in sharing that experience, not in repeating ancient catch-phrases. We can affirm the reality of God in Jesus Christ without a particular time-bound metaphysic.'

A few Muslims have also suggested that some of the difficulty is a matter of language. Sir Sayyid Ahmad Khan (1817-1898), the founder of Indian Islamic modernism, tried to understand the language in its historical setting. 'In the Western world, "father" is a term applied to the originator of something ... the son is he whom God has formed with his hands... If we would express it in Arabic idiom then father means *rabb* (Lord) and "son" *al-'abd al-maqbul* (the chosen servant) and these meanings agree exactly with the application of these terms in the Old and New Testaments'

With reference to 'Son of God' he says,

'Amongst the Greeks it was commonly held that a very holy and reverenced person should be called "Son of God" ... When the disciples intended to spread the Christian religion by means of the Greek language they had to give Christ such a title of honour.'

The Persian writer Shin Parto, in his life of Jesus, *Seven Faces,* writes,

'Christians say that Jesus is Son of God, but it is better to call Him Son of Love, one who was born in love, taught men love and was crucified for love and liberty.'

The Egyptian Khalid M Khalid in *Together on the Road: Muhammad and Jesus,* quotes the Gospel titles "Saviour of the world" and "Bread of Life" and speaks of God as "Father" and says "God is love." In a review of Kenneth Cragg's *The Call of the Minaret,* M. Hamidullah wrote that 'Muslims also admit the exalted position of Jesus, who saw with the eyes of God, talked with the tongue of God, and was absorbed (*fana*) in God, a position which is not incompatible with his not being God but remaining a man, a very exalted man.'

As we have seen, Muslim devotion also gives an exalted position to Muhammad whilst insisting that he too remained a man.

Professor S Vahiduddin, then the Indian Institute of Islamic Studies in New Delhi, some years ago, gave me his article 'What Christ Means to Me.' He wrote that

'The vision of Christ in Muslim experience is indelibly associated with the Virgin Mother and consequently he is referred to as Ibn Maryam, not only in the prophetic tradition but in secular literature. The Qur'an accords pre-eminence to the Virgin Mary among the women of creation.'

Professor Vahiduddin, having drawn attention to Jesus Christ's miracles and healing touch, went on to say,

'Christ reflects in every act of his God's *Jamal* in all its fullness; in other words He is the embodiment of that tender aspect of the divine which the Qur'an calls *rahma.* And this is what Rudolf Otto calls *mysteriosum fascinosum.* The Muslim scripture is fully alert to this aspect of Christ's life and bears witness to the fact that it is in virtue of Christ's tender disposition that God "instilled soft-heartedness and mercy in the hearts of those who followed him (57, 27)."'

In rejecting the divinity of Jesus, Muslims also, as we have seen reject the doctrine of the Trinity. Here, however, especially language more than content seems to be in dispute. Geoffrey Parrinder argues that 'although commentators have taken its words as a rejection of orthodox Christian doctrine, it seems more likely that it is heretical doctrines that are denied in the Qur'an. Parrinder refers to the heresy of Patripassianism that so identified Christ and God as to suggest that God the Father had suffered on the cross. There seems also to have been a tendency by some to treat Christ and Mary as separate gods - teaching rejected by the Qur'an (4, 169-171).

Both religions speak of a God who is in relation to the created world and to humanity, rather than a remote Deity. In his *Call of the Minaret*, Kenneth Cragg suggested that when Christians speak of 'God the Son' they mean 'God in the act of revelation.' To this, S M Tufail, who was a good friend to me in my early years with the World Congress of Faiths, replied that 'the change of persons into attributes is nothing which is derogatory to the internal character of God.' Here is a discussion which needs to be pursued by theologians. At least it suggests that Christians and Muslims could come closer in understanding and in their witness to the One God.

The Death of Jesus

The other main area of dispute is about the death of Jesus. Despite the scholarly consensus that the chief responsibility rests with the Romans, traditional Muslim teaching puts the blame on the Jews - which may appear anti-Semitic. The Jews, it is said, tried to kill Jesus, but were unable to do so. God would not let the Messiah suffer a shameful death so it was only in appearance that Jesus was crucified. In reality, he was raised to the presence of God. This denial is out of respect for Jesus, who is regarded as a prophet. It reflects the dominant Muslim view which we have already discussed that God's cause is guaranteed ultimate success in this world

The key passage, in Richard Bell's translation of the Qur'an is:

'So for their [Jews'] violating their compact, and for their unbelief in the signs of God, their killing the prophets without justification, and for their unbelief, and their speaking against Mary a mighty slander; and for their saying: "We killed the Messiah, Jesus, son of Mary, the messenger of God", though they did not kill him and did not crucify him, but he was counterfeited for them; verily those who have gone different ways in regard to him are in doubt about him; they have no (revealed) knowledge of him and only follow opinion; though they did not certainly kill him. Nay, God raised him to himself. God is sublime, wise. And there is no people of the Book but will say they believe in him before his death, and on the day of resurrection, he will be regarding them a witness.'(4, 156-7)

There are various translations of the phrase that Bell translates as 'he was counterfeited for them.' One reads 'it appeared to them as such'; another as 'only a likeness of that was shown to them.' Sometimes it is suggested that someone else was substituted for Jesus - perhaps Simon of Cyrene or Judas or Pilate - and was crucified in his place. Similar suggestions were already current in some apocryphal gospels. It has also been suggested that Jesus fell into a coma and revived. One heretical sect claims that Jesus after his eventual death died and was buried in Kashmir. The orthodox Muslim view is that Jesus was a true servant of God and that no one could kill the soul. A note in the Saudi Arabian translation observes

'The end of the life of Jesus on earth is as much involved in mystery as his birth... It is not profitable to discuss the many doubts and conjectures among early Christian sects and among Muslim theologians.'

Muslims also reject Christian teaching about the Atonement. Ulfat Aziz-us-Samd in his *Comparative Study of Christianity and Islam* says the doctrine is unsound for three reasons. Man is not born in sin; God does not require a price to forgive the sinner and the idea of a vicarious sacrifice is unjust and cruel. Further, the Qur'an says that no one can take upon himself or herself the sins of another person, because each person will be rewarded or punished according to his or her deserts. In part, I agree with him, and by no means all Christians accept the substitutionary theory of the atonement which holds that Jesus' blood paid the price which humans deserved to pay for their sins. Traditional theories of the atonement stress the objective work of Christ that by his actual historical self-sacrifice, the relationship of God and humankind has been changed for all time. Some liberal Christians, as I do myself, take a more subjective view and say that the crucifixion shows up the nature of human sin and evil and reveals more powerfully than any other event the nature of God as self-giving love. It is a message that can transform a person's self-understanding and their relationship to God.

A few Muslim writers have tried to go beyond disputes about what happened to Jesus on the cross to reflect upon the meaning of his passion, thereby opening up a new and potentially fruitful area of discussion between Muslims and Christians.

In his book *City of Wrong,* Dr Kamel Hussein said that

> 'God raised him [Jesus] unto Him in a way that we can leave unexplained among the several mysteries which we have taken for granted on faith alone.'

Dr Hussein rejects the idea of a substitute and recognises that the intention of the Jews was to kill Jesus. For Dr Kamel Hussein, the meaning of the crucifixion is not dependent on what actually happened. The City of Wrong is Jerusalem which stands for all humankind. The events of Good Friday illustrate what happens when people sin against their conscience. The book ends with the words:

> He was the light of God upon the earth. The people of Jerusalem would have nothing to do with him except to extinguish the light. Whereupon, God has darkened the world around them'.'

Professor Vahiduddin also wrote with sympathy of the events of Good Friday.

> 'What greater ignominy and disgrace is there which Christ has not been made to suffer. But here it is that Christ appears in all his glory, and the world and all that it stands for is exposed in all its vanity. Whether we see the end and the culmination of his earthly course in the Christian or the Muslim perspective, death is not allowed to prevail and Christ appears to be ascending to supreme heights defying death. Perhaps it is due to my Muslim background that what strikes me most is not the suffering through which he passes but his triumph through suffering.

> What looks like defeat, subjection to mortality, the brute success of worldly power and of hard-headed priesthood loose their relevance. Death is vanquished once for all, Christ's life serves as a beacon to those who are laid low, who

"labour and are heavy laden" (Matthew 11, 28). Whenever attempts are made to conceptualise that which by its own nature passes all understanding, interminable controversies and disputes arise. But Christ remains an urphenomenon which will defy conceptualisation.

Such attempts by Muslims sympathetically to enter into the meaning of the cross are still rare. Yet if our emphasis is more on the meaning of the death of the Cross than on historical questions about what actually happened, there is room for Christians and Muslims to bring new insights to each other and to co-operate in the relief of suffering.

Professor Vahiduddin ends his brief article in this way:

'The Qur'anic account of Christ's address to His disciples and their response is highly interesting and deeply significant: "But when Jesus became aware of their disbelief he cried: who will be my helpers in the cause of God? The disciples said: we will be helpers to God" (3, 52).
And how else can we help God, poor mortals as we are, but to promote good and to resist evil and to illumine our life with that all over-riding love which embraces friends and foes alike'.

Chapter 6. THE RESPONSIBLE USE OF POWER.

Islam is called by some of its followers 'The Religion of Peace'. The words *islam* and *salam*, (peace), come from the same root. Yet to many in the West, Islam seems to be identified with war and conflict. One of the sharpest contrasts between Jesus and Muhammad is in their attitude to power and the use of force. But there is less difference, as we shall see, between the teaching of Muslim jurists and Christian theologians. Here is an issue on which it is particularly important than members of both religions seek to distinguish true from false teaching. Nothing probably has done more to discredit religion than its being tainted by violence supposedly carried out in the name of God.

A Society Obedient to God

The Muslim world has probably seen no more conflict than Christendom. Certainly, however, Islam today is identified with some revolutionary movements, but before looking in a subsequent chapter at the contemporary scene, it is helpful to see what Islam teaches about the use of force.

Muslims traditionally do not make a distinction between the sacred and the secular. It is the whole community which should submit to God. Society should be modelled on the Qur'an. In Madina, Muhammad, like the Protestant reformer Calvin in Geneva, tried to shape a society that lived in obedience to God's word. The logic of this position is clear. If God is God, then all life should be lived in obedience to God's Laws.

The early caliphs, although nor successors to Muhammad as messengers of God, were his successors as 'commanders of the faithful.' The early caliphs combined spiritual and temporal leadership - as Christians would understand these terms. Gradually the political rulers of Islam lost their religious aura and the rulers came to be replaced, as the conscience-keepers of the community by the *ulam* or learned men, who had studied the holy law in depth. In time only the first four caliphs came to be regarded as truly orthodox. The Umayyad dynasty (661-750) were seen as a reversion to secular kingship. The Abbasid caliphs, who ruled in Baghdad from 750-1258, had rather more prestige and some called themselves *Khalifat Allah*, or God's deputy or even 'the shadow of God upon earth' - phrases that would have shocked Muhammad. With the loss of effective power by the Abbasids in the tenth century, 'all genuine political authority in the mainstream Muslim tradition was secular,' Edward Mortimer wrote in *Faith and Power in the Politics of Islam*. Developments in the Shi'ite tradition were rather different. In the Sunni world 'virtue and justice', Mortimer adds, 'were no longer regarded as indispensable qualifications of a ruler.' By the eleventh century most of the *ulama* were teaching that obedience was an absolute duty, even to an unjust ruler, since an unjust ruler was better than none at all.

Today some radical Muslims question this divorce between state and religion. They are very critical of the life-style and secular policies of some Muslim rulers and have campaigned, with success in some countries, for the introduction of Shari'a law instead of the law codes which they inherited from Western imperialist rulers. Some of the activists in the 'Arab Spring', however, want a more open and democratic form of government.

As in the early days, many Muslims, where possible, expect to live in an Islamic state. Yet usually where Muslims are a minority, they are taught to obey the laws of the country where they live, but some groups, like the Muslim Parliament in Britain, would hope that their country of residence would in due course become Muslim.

This concern for a society that is obedient to God goes back to the Prophet Muhammad himself. As we have seen, he met with hostility and ridicule in Mecca, but in 622 CE he was invited to become leader of the neighbouring town of Madina. From there, he in due course attacked and captured Mecca. Whether or not he foresaw the quick expansion of Islam that followed his death we do not know, but Islam's military conquests remain some of history's most rapid and enduring victories. There are various economic, social and political factors which contributed to the Prophet's victory and to subsequent Muslim expansion. Our interest here, however, is in his acceptance of power and the use of force. The command of God was 'Recite .' 'Your only duty is to deliver (the message)' God told the Prophet (42, 48). Yet his preaching met with a meagre response. Is it sufficient to proclaim God's message and accept its rejection or should a person use the means available to them to ensure its success? If you are convinced that you have been commissioned by God, it is understandable that you try to effect that divine commission. As Kenneth Cragg put it,

'After thirteen years of sustained and patient witness by word alone, and of relatively scant response within a community proudly resistant and incorrigible, Muhammad determined on emigration. The divine word could not be allowed to fail of "manifest victory". If this was manifestly *not* attained by preaching, then the very loyalty that preached must pass beyond its verbal task into an active accomplishment of "victory."'

The Muslim writer Fazlur Rahman, said,

'Muhammad never lost the hope of success nor, indeed, the dire and stark realization that he was duty-bound to succeed.... It is part of the Qur'anic doctrine that simply to deliver the message, to suffer frustration, and not to succeed, is immature spirituality.'

It needs, however, to be stressed that force was only to be used in self-defence not in propagation of the faith.

Is Force ever justified?

Islam condemns strife, *fasa* and many Muslim writers insist that violence should only be a last resort. It has also been pointed out that the battles of that time were quite small affairs in which probably less than two hundred people in all lost their lives. The Prophet is said not to have spent more than one and a half days in actual fighting in a missionary career of twenty three years.

One can compare Muhammad's choice to that of Jesus who rejected the use of political power and taught the way of non-resistance, although it has to be noted that the political context of their ministries was very different. Cragg notes that the Qur'an makes mention of Moses, David and Abraham as exponents of prophetic action, but that there is no mention of Amos, Hosea, Isaiah or Jeremiah - prophets who chose to suffer rather than compromise with political power. Jesus followed in the tradition of the Suffering Servant. In the Qur'an Isa (Jesus) is a faithful teacher and witness and warner to his people He is not externally 'successful', although as we have seen Muslims believe he was rescued from death and vindicated by the action of God. Some Muslims see Jesus' failure as evidence of Jesus' lesser status as compared to Muhammad.

A comparison to the early history of Sikhism is also interesting. The first Sikh Gurus were pacifist. They suffered intense persecution. Two Gurus and many of their followers were martyred. The tenth Guru, Guru Gobind Singh, however, created the *Khalsa* and organised the community to defend itself. Rather than see themselves and their faith community destroyed, the Sikhs chose to defend themselves and their faith by force.

Muhammad's choice was similar. This highlights the complex question of when and whether it is right for those who are God-fearing to use force. Here is an area which Muslims and Christians need to explore more fully together. Does Truth need to be upheld by force with the inevitable compromises that this entails or is its purity and vulnerability more powerful? Jesus embodies a love that suffers. The only victory is the change of heart won by such self-giving love. The comparison of the choice made by Muhammad and Jesus has clarified my own thinking and deepened my commitment to the way of the Cross, the path of non-resistant suffering love.

I am aware, nonetheless, of the painful choices this too entails. Does it make one appear to stand aside in the face of evil and terrible suffering? This would be the criticism of many Muslims. Ibn Khaldun Ibn Khaldun (1332-1402), who was born in Tunis and moved to Granada and then to Cairo, a distinguished historian and philosopher, who has been called 'the father of sociology', said that verbal propagation of a faith is incomplete. He did not consider Christianity to be a 'missionary' religion precisely because it had no *jihad*.

The majority of Christians have rejected the way of Jesus as unrealistic. The early Christians were pacifist and in every age some Christians, usually a minority, have held to this belief. The majority, however, have accepted the doctrine, in various forms, of the just war. The theory requires, first, that there is a just cause, which may be self-defence or the protection of the weak and vulnerable, the recovery of something wrongfully taken, or the punishment of evil. Secondly, war should be initiated by a legitimate authority. Thirdly, those involved should have a right intention. Fourthly, the force should be proportional to the objectives. The teaching also tried to limit the cruelties of war. At the time of the Reformation, there was considerable debate about whether revolution could be justified. Some Christians held that it was right to rebel against a tyrant.

Limitations on the Use of Force

The teaching of the Qur'an and of Muslim jurists is similar. The use of force is allowed, but only in certain clearly defined situations of self-defence or to protect innocent victims. Efforts should also be made to limit the cruelties of war. The Qur'an says;

To those against whom
War is made, permission
Is given (to fight), because
They are wronged; - and verily,
Allah is Most Powerful
For their aid;-
(They are) those who have
Been expelled from their homes
In defiance of right, -
(For no cause) except
That they say, "Our Lord Is Allah."
Did not Allah
Check one set of people
By means of another,
There would surely have been
Pulled down monasteries, churches,
Synagogues, and mosques, in which
The name of Allah is commemorated
In abundant measure.
Allah will Certainly aid those who
Aid His (cause); for verily
Allah is Full of Strength,
Exalted in Might,
(Able to enforce His Will).

(They are) those who,
If We establish them
In the land, establish
Regular prayer and give
Zakat, enjoin
The right and forbid wrong.
With Allah rests the end
(And decision) of (all) affairs. (22, 39-41).

The Qur'an says also that:

And did not Allah

Check one set of people
By means of another,
The earth would indeed
Be full of mischief:
But Allah is full of bounty
To all the worlds' (2, 251).

The Qur'an describes war as a conflagration and God's aim is to put it out. 'Every time they kindle the fire of war, Allah doth extinguish it. (5, 64). The Qur'an tries to limit the evils of war. If the enemy stops fighting, Muslims should do the same, because 'Allah is Oft-Forgiving, Most Merciful.'(2, 191).although, this verse follows the rather chilling verse that begins:

And slay them
Wherever ye catch them,
And turn them out from
From where they have
Turned you out;
For Persecution
is worse than slaughter. (2, 191).

This is an example of the importance of reading a verse in context. The injunction in verse 191 is only valid in the context of hostilities in progress - rather like the military command to 'shoot to kill'. It should be understood, as the Saudi Arabian translation comments, in the awareness that in general 'Islam is the religion of peace, goodwill, mutual understanding, and good faith. But it will not acquiesce in wrong-doing, and its men will hold their lives cheap in defence of honour, justice, and the religion which they hold sacred.'

Cruelty such as disfiguring the enemy dead or torturing prisoners is forbidden. Plundering was forbidden and also unnecessary damage - for example cutting down fruit-trees was forbidden

When an enemy combatant was about to be killed by Usama bin Zaid, he declared his faith in Islam. Usama killed him nevertheless. The Prophet was greatly displeased and questioned Usama, who said that the man was not sincere. The Prophet retorted 'Had you cut open his heart to make sure whether he was sincere or not?' Yet, Muhammad was well aware of the ambiguities of power and the insincerity that it could cause. When a group of Bedouins came to him and said, 'We believe', the Qur'an gives as the reply,

'Ye have no faith; but ye
(Only) say "We have submitted
Our wills to Allah."
For not yet has Faith
Entered your hearts.' (49, 14).

The Qur'an uses the word *islam* in two senses. One is a personal and religious 'submission' to God. The other is a visible political 'submission' to Islam.

The Qur'an accepts that it is legitimate to use power in establishing a community obedient to God. God's approval was shown by God's gift of victory. Success or 'manifest victory' was seen as a sign of God's favour. This was evident at the battle at Badr, where, despite being heavily outnumbered, the Muslims were victorious. (3, 13) When the following year, the Muslims were unsuccessful at Uhud, this was explained as a result of Muslim disobedience. It did not alter the conviction that God's will is sovereign. If, therefore, the Muslim cause is just, God will in the end uphold it - even if for a time the Muslims suffer testing and punishment. So some religiously motivated Muslim Palestinians reject compromise with Israel, believing that their cause is just and that therefore God will in the end vindicate them.

Jihad

The use of force, therefore, in certain circumstances, is justified in Islam and it is in this context that the word *jihad* is to be understood. The word *jihad* means striving, especially striving in the cause of God. It is personal commitment to God's service. al-Jilani, also known as Abd al-Qadir al-Jili (1077-1166), founder of the Qadiriya Sufi Order quotes the Prophet as saying , 'We have returned from the lesser *jihad* to the greater *jihad.*' - meaning that the purifying of the inner self is more important than the physical struggle against the enemies of Islam. *Jihad* involves a personal struggle against evil and the use of intellect and speech in support of right and truth and the correction of wrong and evil. Too often this wider meaning is forgotten and the word is confined to the use of force. War is primarily the responsibility of the community, not the individual. This is why, except by the Kharijites, who were an early schismatic puritanical group, *jihad* is not regarded as one of the pillars of Islam.

Jihad is often taken to mean 'religious' war, but this is misleading. Certainly it does not imply the killing of non-believers just because of their lack of faith. The Qur'an makes clear that 'there can be no compulsion in religion: Truth stands out clear from Error.' (2, 256). Non-believers who were willing to submit should be accepted and as we shall see there was special provision for the Christians and Jews.

Islamic teaching normally only allows war under three conditions. The first is to oppose and expel those who attack Muslims without just cause.

'Will you not fight people
Who violated their oaths
Plotted to expel the Messenger
And attacked you First? (9, 13).

The second condition is to prevent oppression and persecution of the faithful. This may be extended to the protection of those who are not Muslim but who are victims of unjustified aggression.

'And why should you not
Fight in the cause of Allah
And of those who, being weak,
Are ill-treated (and oppressed)? -
Men, women, and children,
Whose cry is "Our Lord!
Rescue us from this town
Whose people are oppressors;
And raise for us from Thee
One who will protect;
And raise for us from Thee
One who will help" (4, 75)'

Thirdly, force could be used, as we have seen above, to protect places intended for the worship of God - not only mosques, but also churches and synagogues. (22, 40).

Perhaps the most influential analysis of war was made by Ibn Khaldun. He held that war was not an accidental calamity or disease but was rooted in the selfishness and anger of human beings. He distinguished four kinds of war: tribal wars, feuds and raids, *jihad* and wars against rebels and dissenters. The first two are wars of disobedience and not justified, whereas the other two are wars of obedience and justified. Victory, he held, depended on military preparedness and spiritual insight.

Muslim jurists submitted *jihad* to close analysis.

(a) *Jihad* against polytheists is in some verses of the Qur'an encouraged. For example, 9, 5, says, 'fight pagans wherever you may find them', but these are pagans who do not abide by treaties to which they have agreed. 9, 123 is similar, but as the notes in the Saudi Arabian translation say 'When conflict becomes inevitable ... mealy mouthed compromises are not right for soldiers of truth.' 47, 4 says the same, but adds that when the Unbelievers have been subdued

> Bind (the captives) Firmly: Thereafter (Is the time for) either
> Generosity (freedom without ransom) or ransom:
> Until the war lays down its burdens.

(b) *Jihad* against believers was sub-divided by the jurist al-Mawardi (972-1058) into:

(i) *Jihad* against believers. Apostates could become subject to *jihad*. After Muhammad's death, some Arab tribes attempted to secede. Abu Bakr gave them solemn warning after which they were attacked with fire and sword.

(ii) *Jihad* against dissension. When the Kharijites, rejecting Caliph 'Ali's offer of peaceful relations and permission to pray in the mosque, continued in their opposition to the Caliph, he overwhelmed them at the battle of Nahruwan in 658 CE.

(iii) *Jihad* against bandits, who were to be severely punished, unless they repented.

(c) *Jihad* against the People of the Book A Jews Christian or Zoroastrians A could either embrace Islam, and become a full citizen or, if he retained his beliefs, provided he accepted the authority of the imam and paid taxes, he would be tolerated as a Dhimmi, with somewhat restricted rights of citizenship.

(d) *ribat* or strengthening of the frontiers was accepted by some jurist as allowable. This was based on the verse, 8, 60:

> 'Against them [Unbelievers] make ready
> Your strength to the utmost
> Of your power, including
> Weapons of war, to strike terror
> Into (the hearts) of the enemies.'

But immediately, the next verse continues,

But if the enemy
Incline towards peace,
Do thou (also) incline
Towards peace, and trust in Allah. (8, 61).

Normally *ribat* was interpreted defensively, in the hope that it would prevent conflict.

Although the Prophet is reported to have said that 'He who supports a tyrant or oppressor knowing he is a tyrant casts himself outside the pale of Islam', Al-Ash'ari (873-935) and Din ibn Jama'a (d. 1333) forbade uprisings against tyrants.

There were also rules about who should participate and about the conduct of war. Fighters should be adult males who were believers. Non-combatants should be spared unless they actively helped the enemy. Before the first Syrian campaign, Abu Bakr read ten rules that limited violence. For example, soldiers were told not to slaughter a sheep or a camel except for eating, not to burn bees, and not to cut down trees with fruit on them. The Prophet had already forbidden killing a decrepit old man, or a small child or a woman. Some of the jurists, however, greatly limited the scope of these prohibitions and Abu Hanifa (1699-767) said that all is permitted against the enemy.

Arbitration was encouraged, based on verse 4, 59, especially to solve disputes within Islam. Muhammad had also submitted to arbitration in a dispute with the Jewish Banu Qurayza tribe. This provided a precedent for the use of arbitration between Muslims and non-Muslims when questions of faith were not in dispute.

It can be seen that Muslim discussion of *jihad* is not dissimilar to the Christian teaching about a just war. Islam accepts the use of force in self-defence, to defend religion and to protect the weak. The need now is to see how these rules apply to the United Nations' peace-keeping role. When is it right for the international community to intervene to protect the weak and, for example, to try to prevent genocide? What cost in civilian casualties is acceptable? How do you impose sanctions without hurting the most vulnerable members of the population of a country? To what extent can peace-keeping forces intervene in civil war? There are important issues for members of different faiths to discuss together with politicians and generals.

Of course, the teachings of both Islam and Christianity have not always been observed and rulers have been tempted to declare a war of self-interest to be a *jihad* or a just war. It is important also to recognise that in much of both Christian and Muslim history religion has been part of a community's self-identity. As a result a conflict acquires religious overtones, although its cause is not really religious differences. There is, therefore, a clear responsibility on religious leaders to distance themselves from this misuse of religion. They need courage to challenge their own community when they indulge needlessly in violence or the abuse of human rights.

A step in this direction was taken at the Millennium World Peace Summit of Religious and Spiritual Leaders which met in UN General Assembly Hall in August 2000. The religious leaders agreed a 'Commitment to Global Peace' which included a rejection of killing in the name of God. There are, of course, those including suicide bombers who claim to fight in the name of God, but religious leaders need to make clear that they do not have the endorsement of the faithful.

There is a clear difference between Muhammad and Jesus' attitude to the use of power, but much less difference between the teaching and practice of Christendom and the world of Islam. It may be true today that rulers in Muslim states make more specific reference to Islam than most European leaders do to Christianity, but the real causes of conflict is usually about economic and political disputes rather than primarily about religion. Religion is called in to give respectability to policies decided on quite other grounds. The crimes of individuals, however, as the Muslim scholar K G Saiyadain wrote in *World Religions and World Peace* should not be blamed 'on their respective religions. In judging a religion, we should do so as it is at its best and in the context of its genuine teachings.'

If both Christians and Muslims have, in some situations, accepted the use of force, their major contribution should be in creating a climate of trust and peace. The dialogue between the faithful is itself a contribution but members of both religions need also to emphasise the teachings of their respective religions which make for peace.

Here the Sufi tradition of Islam has a particular contribution to make with its emphasis on the spiritual *jihad* as well as the teachings of peace. Dr Hasan Askari, who worked for a time at the Centre for Christian-Muslim Relations at Birmingham gave a talk some years ago on 'Muslim Approaches to Religious Sources for Peace.' He began by reference to Prayer which is central to a Muslim's life. 'To invoke the One is to become one, to rise above all division and discord. To invoke the name of God is to be in His Presence: and to be in His Presence is to be in a perpetual state of prayer, and therefore *prayer is an actualisation of peace.*' Askari then admitted that religious dogmatism is a fertile breeding ground of hatred and fear, but that acknowledgement of the transcendence of the One God brought people together beyond religious divisions. Members of different religions were called by God to strive 'as in a race in all virtues.' (5, 48). Striving for peace, Askari, continued is to struggle for justice, which is the prerequisite for peace, and to oppose corruption and disorder.

Muhammad Raceme Boa Muhaiyaddeen, a Sufi from Sri Lanka, in his *Islam and World Peace*, published after his death, also stressed the inner *jihad.*

'For man to raise his sword against man, for man to kill man, is not holy war. True holy war is to praise God and to cut away the enemies of truth within our own hearts. We must cast out all that is evil within us, all that opposes God. This is the war that we must fight.'

The Oneness of God, he taught, means also that we never see another person as separate from ourselves. As Jesus said, we should 'love our neighbour just as much as we love ourselves.'

I am not aware of ever having chosen to sing 'Onward Christian soldiers,' and no doubt congregations where I have been in charge have felt deprived. The imagery of warfare applied to the spiritual life has its dangers. Too easily one identifies the enemy with opponents rather than one's own inner temptations to sin and even more dangerously those opponents can be demonized and seen as God's enemies as well as our own. The cruelty of the Crusades is not forgotten in the Muslim world.

If Christians are uneasy with the militant language used by some Muslims today, they need to acknowledge that some Christians in the past and still today find a similar message in Christianity. Those of us who disown that Christian tradition and emphasise the message of God's forgiving love will be glad that in Islam too there is a similar strand. Here again the issue today is 'what is true religion?' Those of every faith who believe that the divine will is love and forgiveness and that peace can only come through reconciliation have to stand together against those who find in their religion a call to victory and triumph over the infidel. Evil needs to be resisted, but the true victory is the conversion of the wrong-doer.

Chapter 7. SUFFERING

In Islam there is the confidence that in the end God will vindicate the righteous, whereas, it has been suggested above, Christianity, to which the Cross of Christ is so central, has a more tragic view of life. This contrast, as we shall see is not entirely true, especially when the Shi'ite tradition is considered. Even so, Christianity has probably given a larger place to redemptive suffering than Islam. The question of the suffering of the faithful, nevertheless, has been a concern for Muslims just as much as for Christians.

The Qur'an opens with the words, 'In the name of Allah, the Beneficent, the Merciful.' These words are found at the head of almost every chapter or *sura.* Equally, the Qur'an affirms that God is omnipotent, the Lord of the Universe and the Lord of history. God's ultimate responsibility for all that happens is recognised. 'Allah has power over all things.' (35, 1; 2, 106)

Suffering, therefore, in a sense comes from God. 'No kind of calamity can occur, except by the leave of Allah.' (64, 11). The question then is why God allows suffering. There is a tendency in Islam to see success or 'manifest victory' as a sign of God's favour. When at the battle of Badr, the Muslims, who were largely outnumbered, won an important victory over the Meccans, this was taken as a sign of God's approval.

'There has Already been
For you a Sign
In the two armies
That met (in combat).
One was fighting in the Cause
Of Allah, the other
Resisting Allah; these saw
With their own eyes
Twice their own number
But Allah doth support
With his aid whom He pleaseth.
In this is a lesson
For such as have eyes to see.' (3,13).

Yet the following year, at Uhud, the Muslims failed to repeat their success. Why was this?

'Not for thee, (but for Allah),
Is the decision:
Whether He turn in mercy
To them, or punish them;
For they are indeed wrong-doers.
To Allah belongeth all
That is in the heavens
And on earth.
He forgiveth whom He pleaseth;
And punisheth whom He pleaseth;
But Allah is Oft-Forgiving,
Most Merciful.' (3, 129)

In effect the answer in Islam is 'submission', acceptance of the will of God, with whom it is not for us to argue. But experience of life led to some thinkers wrestling with the problem of why the faithful are not always successful. Various answers were suggested, although the general expectation remained that the faithful would be victorious. The rapid and triumphant spread of Islam seemed to confirm this.

Suffering may be a punishment, especially of proud and evil men. It is said of Pharaoh, who refused to listen to Moses and let the people of Israel leave Egypt.

When at length they
Provoked us, We exacted
Retribution upon them and
We drowned them all.
And we made them
(A People) of the Past
And an Example
To later ages.' (43, 55-6.)

Although suffering may be a punishment, it should not be assumed this is necessarily true of the sufferings of others. For example, those who die in battle should not be derided as though survivors enjoyed the special favour of God. Equally one should not assume that the unfortunate are being punished by God and so ignore their needs

'It is no fault in the blind
Nor in one born lame, nor

In one afflicted with illness.' (24, 61)

In the case of the faithful, suffering may be a correction or a trial or a test.

'Every soul shall have
A taste of death;
And we test you
By evil and by good
By way of trial.
To us must ye return.' (21, 35)

Again the Qur'an says,

'Be sure we shall test you
With something of fear
And hunger, some loss
In goods, lives and the fruits
(Of your toil), but give
Glad tidings to those
Who patiently persevere, -
Who say, when afflicted
With calamity: "To Allah
We belong, and to Him
Is our return."' (2, 155-6).

The Qur'an recognises that are those who are religious because they hope to be rewarded.

'There are among men
Some who serve Allah,
As it were, on the verge.
If good befalls them, they are
Therewith, well content; but
If a trial comes to them,
They turn on their faces:
They lose both this world
And the Hereafter: that
is indeed the evident loss.' (22, 11).

Testing is, therefore, to be expected - particularly of the faithful.

'If a wound hath touched you,
Be sure a similar wound
Hath touched the others.
Such days (of varying fortunes)
We give to men and men
By turns; that Allah may know
Those that believe,
And that He may take
To Himself from your ranks
Martyr-witnesses (to Truth)...
Did ye think that ye
Would enter Heaven
Without Allah testing
Those of you who fought hard
(In His Cause) and
Remained steadfast? (3, 140-142).

Again the Qur'an says:

'Do men think that
They will be left alone
On saying "We believe",
And that they will not
Be tested?' (29, 2)

There is then an 'instrumental' view of suffering. God uses it to punish and to test. This affirms the conviction that God is in control and that suffering can be part of God's merciful providence to bring people to a right way of living. God does not test people beyond their capability (2, 286) and always offers them the possibility of repentance and forgiveness. The proper response is patience and endurance and trust in God. God in the end will reward the faithful and punish unbelievers. (2, 80-82).

Sometimes outsiders have thought of Islam as fatalistic, but this is a misreading of the Qur'an. The Qur'an makes clear that suffering as far as possible should be relieved and its causes removed. One way of doing so is to construct a society based on the teaching of the Qur'an and this is why some Muslims want an Islamic state. The fashioning of an Islamic society was intended to alleviate suffering. In early Muslim societies the position of women and slaves was improved compared to their contemporaries; almsgiving was required and limitations were placed on war and vengeance.

Equally the individual Muslim was expected to be compassionate. In a passage, which is sometimes thought to refer to Muhammad himself, the Qur'an says,

'Did He not find thee
An orphan and give thee
Shelter? (and care)?
And he found thee
Wandering, and He gave
Thee guidance.
And He found thee
In need, and made
Thee independent
Therefore, treat not
The orphan with harshness,
Nor repulse him who asks,
But the Bounty of thy Lord -
Rehearse and proclaim.' (93, 6-11).

Sometimes acts of mercy are valued above ritual. The Qur'an says:

It is not righteousness
That ye turn your faces
Towards East or West,
But it is righteousness
To believe in Allah
And the Last Day
And the Angels,
And the Book,
And the messengers
To spend your substance,
Out of love for Him
For your kin,
For orphans,
For the needy,
For the wayfarer,
For those who ask,

And for the ransom of slaves;
To be steadfast in prayer,
And give Zakat,[charitable tax]
To fulfil contracts
Which ye have made;
And to be firm and patient,
In pain (or suffering)
And adversity,
And throughout
All periods of panic.
Such are the people
Of the truth, the God-fearing.(2, 177).

The teaching of the Qur'an, in brief, suggests that success should attend the faithful, but if not it may be a punishment for evil or a test of faith. Suffering does not lead to a questioning of God's power or mercy. Muslims, moreover, should seek to alleviate suffering, both individually and by creating a just Islamic society.

Yet there are unanswered questions. Does the stress on divine omnipotence allow adequately for human free will? This became a subject of major philosophical debate. The classical theologians of Islam tried to hold together both divine authority and human responsibility. The Qur'an and *hadith* stress the omnipotence of God and some Muslims came close to a determinism which seemed to eclipse human freedom. There was a reaction in a school of thought known as Qadariyya, who held that human beings initiate their own actions and thus determine their destiny. They argued that God remained in control, but that he delegated actions and responsibility to human beings.

The Qadariyya, however, were bitterly attacked for giving too much independence to humans and were called dualists. Orthodox thinkers tried to solve the problem by a concept of 'acquisition' rather than 'delegation'. God did not delegate powers: rather humans acquired them and made them their own. The disciples of al-Ashari (873-935) - the founder of theolgy (*kalam*) - said that God creates in humans the resolve to do something. Humans have no effective, but only an acquisitive part in the deed - that is to say human beings do not *cause* something to happen but rather connect human power with the deed. This really still allows for the complete control of God, but al-Ashari seems to have modified this extreme position by saying it is possible to allow evil without being its immediate or direct cause. For example, Abel by refusing to defend himself 'willed' or did not prevent his own murder, but he did not cause it.

While God is the source of blessing, humans are responsible for their misfortunes:

'Whatever good, (O man!)
Happens to thee, is from Allah
But whatever evil happens
To thee, is from thyself '(4, 79)

Yet not everything that a person considers as 'evil fortune' is bad in its consequences. As the Qur'an says:

'But it is possible
That ye dislike a thing
Which is good for you,
And that ye love a thing
Which is bad for you.' (2, 216).

God is essentially inscrutable - that is what submission means. God cannot be put under any necessity - not even moral necessity. Al-Ashari, apparently, said,

'God is Lord of creation. He does what He wishes and effects what He desires. If He sent all beings to paradise there would be no injustice, or if He sent them all to Gehenna there would be no wrong. Wrong doing means disposing of things not one's own or putting them in the wrong place. But since God is the owner of all things without exception, it is impossible to think of wrong-doing in connection with Him and it is impossible to attribute injustice to Him.'

Paul likewise, in the *Letter to the Romans*, he compares God to a potter. 'Nay but, O man, who art thou that repliest against God? Shall the thing formed say to him that formed it, Why hast thou made me thus? Hath not the potter power over the clay, of the same lump to make one vessel unto honour, and another unto dishonour? (9, 20-21).

Personally I have some difficulties with this argument, because God is surely always more moral than human beings.

Christians may ask whether Islam allows sufficiently for the tragic dimension in life. There is no doctrine of original sin and so no need for an act of atonement. Shi'ite Muslims, however, out of their own tragic history had to contend with the fact that the faithful, even over time, were not vindicated in this world.

Shi'ite Perspectives

The division between Shi'ite and Sunni Muslims centred on who should be Caliph. When Muhammed died he was succeeded by Abu Bakr, whose faithfulness to Muhammad was unfailing and whose daughter, Muhammad had married. Shi'ites hold that Ali, Muhammad's closest relation, who eventually became Caliph, should have been Caliph immediately after Muhammad's death. They, therefore, regard the first three Caliphs were usurpers. Ali's caliphate ended tragically. He was assassinated by a member of the break-away group of Kharijites. Ali's elder son, al-Hasan succeeded him, but publicly renounced the Caliphate in favour of Mu'awiyya. al-Hasan's brother al-Husain, however, refused to renounce his claims in favour of Yazid, who had by then succeeded his father Mu'awiyya. On the way to join his supporters, al-Husain was intercepted by a patrol and surrounded at Karbala. He refused to surrender and on 10th Muharranm 61 AH (10 October 680 CE) his small band were attacked. They resisted, but Husain refused to do so. He and his followers were massacred. A report to Yazid said laconically, 'It did not last long, just time to slay a camel and take a nap.'

According to a tradition, Jesus with his disciples when roaming in the wilderness came upon Karbala, the place where Husain was to die. On the exact spot where he was to be killed, a lion blocked Jesus' path. Jesus spoke to the animal, who replied that on this spot the descendant of Muhammad would be killed and that he would not let Jesus pass until he had cursed his murderers. Another tradition says that a group of gazelles were grazing in Karbala and were lamenting Husain's death and that Jesus then had a vision of the future tragic event and described it vividly.

The deaths of Husain, Ali and even of Hasan were soon seen as martyrdoms and this introduced a new element into Muslim understanding of suffering. Indeed the death of Husain was seen as a cosmic event around which the history of the world revolves. Manifest success could no longer be taken as proof of divine approval. Each year the death of Husain is commemorated. He is 'innocence personified' and sums up all sorrow of Jacob, in the Old Testament, mourning for Joseph, or of Rachel weeping for her children and indeed the suffering of all victims of cruel tyrants. All evil is there at his killing. Husain represents all innocent victims. His suffering, which was totally undeserved, has a virtue which can be pleaded by those burdened with sin and suffering. Thus in the Shi'ite tradition, the ideas of vicarious suffering and martyrdom developed.

There are many forms of Shi'ite passion plays, but the purpose of them all is to encourage actors and spectators to enter into the events as they are re-created and so recognise the benefits of innocent suffering. In one such play, Husain, as he died, prayed to be granted 'bountifully, the key of the treasure of intercession.' Then, at the end of the play, Gabriel delivers a message from Muhammad. 'None has suffered the pain and afflictions which Husain has undergone. None has, like him, been obedient in my service. As he has taken no steps, save in sincerity, in all that he has done, thou must put the key of Paradise in his hand. The privilege of making intercession for sinners is exclusively his. Husain is, by my peculiar grace, the mediator for all.' In Sunni Islam however, only the Prophet Muhammad is believed to have the capacity to intercede on behalf of those who make supplication.

In his fascinating book *Redemptive Suffering in Islam,* the scholar Dr Mahmoud Ayoub, who was born in a Shi'ite village in South Lebanon, suggests that for the People of God this world is a place of suffering and sorrow, indeed 'the House of Sorrows.' Although, as he says, Islam has stressed the good things of life which a person should thankfully enjoy, he states that a sense of the sorrowfulness of life is equally recognised in Islam, although this may not be the dominant mood of the Qur'an.

The *Hadiths* suggest that the person of faith may expect to be visited with suffering and calamity in accordance with the strength and durability of his faith. When Sa'd b.Abi Waqqas asked the Prophet who were most likely to be afflicted with calamity, he was told, 'The prophets, then the pious, everyone according to the degree of his piety. A man is afflicted according to his faith (*din*); if his faith is durable, his affliction is accordingly increased... until they leave him walking on the face of the earth without any sin cleaving to him.' On another occasion, the Prophet said, 'If God loves a people, He visits them with afflictions. He who is content [with God's will], with him will God be pleased.' There is also this saying in the *Book of Ali,* which Mahmoud Ayoub quotes, 'truly affliction is nearer to the pious man of faith than is fallen rain to the earth.'

Suffering is a purifying test and the person who endures it helps the redemption of others. 'Suffering', writes Mahmoud Ayoub, 'whatever its cause and nature may be, must be regarded as an evil power of negation and destruction. It is non-being, the opposite of the Good which is Being in all its fullness. Suffering or non-being, cannot itself be destroyed, but it can and must be transformed. The transformation of suffering from a power of total negation into something of value is effected through human faith and divine mercy. Thus transformed, suffering becomes the great teacher for the pious, their road to salvation. The redemptive power of suffering lies in the fact that suffering can be overcome only by its own power. This is movingly stated in the Christian liturgical hymn which triumphantly proclaims "Christ rose from the dead, trampling death and giving life to those in the tomb"'.

'Suffering' Mahmoud Ayoub says 'can lead to the annihilation, both physical and spiritual, of the sufferer. But we have argued that ultimate victory over evil, suffering and death, can only be achieved through suffering and death. In fact, where redemption is the primary goal of the life of the religious community, it is accepted as a divine gift of eternal life granted through death. The Christian case is one of the most powerful examples of the phenomenon in human history. We would like to argue that this quest for salvation, in different forms to be sure, plays a major role in the religious life of the Ithna'ashari Shi'ia community.

One aspect of the tradition emphasises Husain's mercy, forgiveness and healing. Some modern writers see the main message of his death to be that of his courage, piety and self-sacrifice. Other writers suggest that Husain died 'in protest against the hunger of the hungry, the poverty of the poor and the oppression of the oppressed.' A play performed in Cairo in 1970 depicted Husain as a revolutionary hero and great martyr. At the end of the play Husain appeared and told the audience:

'Remember me as you struggle in order that justice may reign over you, remember me in your struggle ...When the song of brotherhood disappears and when the poor complain and the pockets of the rich bulge, remember me... Remember my revenge so that you may exact it from tyrants... But if you hold your peace against deception and accept humiliation, then I would be slain anew... I would be killed whenever men are subjugated and humiliated... Then would the wound of the martyr forever curse you because you did not avenge the blood of the martyr. Avenge the blood of the martyr.'

The same event can be remembered by the faithful to teach very different lessons. The Martyrdom of Husain can be used to rally the faithful to seek revenge against those who tyrannise the afflicted, so that Husain becomes, as it were, a prophet of liberation theology! His martyrdom may also be used to teach patience under the purifying test of suffering.

Rumi

Some of the Sufis, mystics who themselves often suffered fierce opposition and even martyrdom, also spoke of the purifying discipline of pain as a way to bring the soul closer to God.

Jalalud Din Rumi wrote,

'When you fall ill and suffer pain, your conscience is awakened,
You are stricken with remorse and pray God to forgive your trespasses.
The foulness of your sin is shown to you, you resolve to come back
to the right way. You promise and vow that henceforth your chosen course of
action will be obedience. Note, then, this principle, O seeker,
pain and suffering make one aware of God.'

The Mystery of Suffering

No religion gives an entirely adequate answer to the mystery of suffering. The attempts to explain it are similar in Islam and Christianity. Christians believe that God in Jesus Christ has entered into and shared human suffering. Further, Christians believe that by his own suffering even to death, Jesus Christ achieved the salvation of the world. Suffering for Christians, therefore, has redemptive possibilities. This note is also to be heard in Islam, but not so loudly. Some Muslims feel that an undue stress on the redemptive quality of suffering may lead to a pietistic indifference to the suffering in the world. Muslims may, therefore, help to remind Christians of their calling to work and pray for God's kingdom of justice. The dialogue of Muslims and Christians may help both to maintain a balance between a recognition of the redemptive possibilities of suffering and the responsibility to do all that is possible to relieve it.

Chapter 7. REPENTANCE AND FORGIVENESS

'There will be no peace in the world without peace between religions.' This maxim of Hans Küng is well known. Recently I heard a Muslim friend add to it, 'There will be no peace in the world without justice' and 'there will be no justice without forgiveness'. His remark stands in sharp contrast to the impression of many in the West that Islam is a harsh and punitive religion - an impression fuelled by reports of women being stoned for adultery or thieves having a hand chopped off or criminals being flogged in some Islamic states.

These practices are condemned by many Muslims, who also condemn acts of terrorism. The popular impression of Islam in the West is unfair, as I have been at pains to point out. Almost every chapter of the Qur'an begins with the words, 'In the name of God the Compassionate, the Merciful.' Even so, I have to admit that I was surprised when I read Mahmoud Ayoub's words in his contribution to *Repentance: a Comparative Perspective* that 'Repentance is an essential element of the Qur'anic world view' or again that 'repentance is one of the fundamental principles of Qur'anic theology and worldview.'

The word most often used in the Qur'an for repentance is *tawbah.* Its basic meaning is turning. 'Legally it signifies turning to God for forgiveness of a sin or act of disobedience. Its primary sense,' Mahmoud Ayub explained, 'is of turning to God as a personal act of love and devotion - and not necessarily from a state of sin. This is a more exalted and deeper level of repentance.' The Prophet Muhammad, for example, whom Muslims believe to have been protected from all sin by God, is said to have declared 'I turn to God every day seventy times.' Repentance is more than just asking for forgiveness, it is a turning to God with sincere love and devotion. It includes awe in the presence of the Holy One, awareness of sin and genuine remorse for it, regret over lost opportunities and a desire to amend one's life. Yet this change of heart, as the Qur'an makes clear, can itself only be achieved by divine grace. Two other Arabic words used for repentance emphasise this wider meaning. *Awbah* has the sense of repeated returning to God with humility, devotion and praise and *inabah* signifies turning to God for help in total submission to his will.

The Qur'an has more than ninety words for sin or offences against God or fellow human beings. Yet there is no doctrine of original sin, although the human propensity to do evil is clearly recognised. As a just and moral sovereign, God is severe in punishment, but more important his mercy is repeatedly affirmed. 'God is Oft-forgiving and Most Merciful' (5, 98). To despair of God's infinite mercy is itself a grave sin. God says in the Qur'an, 'O my servants who have transgressed against their souls, despair not of the Mercy of Allah, for Allah forgives all sins.' (39, 53). It is a verse which is reminiscent of the sentiments in the hymn 'Wilt thou forgive that sin?' written by the seventeenth century metaphysical poet John Donne. The poet lists his various sins which need forgiveness and then in a final verse confesses,

'I have a sin of fear, that when I've spun
My last thread, I shall perish on the shore;
But swear by thyself, that at my death thy Son
Shall shine, as he shines now and heretofore:
And, having done that, thou hast done:
I fear no more.'

God's mercy is affirmed in the *hadith* or traditions. It is said that 'When God created the universe, He prescribed with His own hand for Himself, "my mercy shall overcome my wrath"'. Interestingly, in the Jewish tradition, the Talmud says, '"What does the Holy One, blessed be He, pray?" Rav Zutra bar Tovi said in the name of Rav, "May it be My will that My mercy suppresses My anger and that My mercy will prevail over My other attributes, so that I may deal with My children in the attribute of mercy and on their behalf, stop short of the limit of strict justice."'

Tradition in Islam speaks of God seeking the sinner and rejoicing at his repentance, as two examples vividly illustrate. In one it is said that

'God is more joyful at the repentance of His servant when He returns to Him than one of you would be if had taken his she-camel with his food and drink into an arid desert. She runs away from him, and he despairs of ever finding her. In desperation, he falls asleep in the shade of a tree. But when he awakes, he finds her standing beside him. With exceeding joy, he rushes to take her by the rope.'

In another passage it is said,

'God is more joyful at the repentance of His servant than a sterile man or woman who begets a child, an erring person who finds the right path, and a thirsty person who accidentally comes upon a source of refreshing water.'

On one occasion Muhammad, according to one of the Companions, Anas, said,

'Allah says: "When a servant of Mine advances to me by a foot, I advance to him by a yard and when he advances towards Me a yard, I advance towards him the length of his arms' spread. When he comes to me walking, I go to him running."'

Repentance or turning to God is prominent in the Sufi tradition. For the famous Persian Sufi master Hujwiri (d. c.1077), it is the first station of the traveller on the way to truth. For Sufis, the mystical life is a journey from God to the world of created things and back to God the creator of all things. This journey consists of acts of worship and obedience and a turning from carnal and worldly temptations. There is an ascetic strain in Sufism but also a deep sense of the love and mercy of God. Repentance is the means by which one is turned towards God. As Shaykh Ibrahim al-Daqqaq (d.1015 or 1021) said, 'Repentance means that you should be to God a face without a back even as you have formerly been unto him a back without a face.'

The Shi'ite tradition with its more pessimistic view of human life sees sin as a primary cause of life's troubles. Repentance, as Mahmoud Ayoub says, has therefore a redemptive significance and can help to lessen the evils in the world. Repentance should be expressed publicly through penitential liturgies.

Although there is much in Islam about God's mercy, there is also clear teaching about a day of Judgement, when each person's deeds will be weighed on an exact balance (7,8; 21, 47; 23, 103f; 101, 6-9) and the book of the record for each person will be opened (10, 61; 17, 13f;). No one can help someone else: each person is responsible for their own actions. Yet the possibility of intercession especially by Muhammad and later by angels and martyrs came to be accepted and modified this strict accounting.

The faithful are promised in the Qur'an the pleasures of affluence. 'You and your spouses will enter Paradise and be glad. You will be served with golden plates and goblets. Everything the heart desires and that pleases the eye will be there, where you will abide forever.' (43, 70- 71). Men will enjoy virgins with lovely eyes and swelling breasts (44, 54; 52, 20; 55, 72-76; 56, 34-37; 78, 33). The great theologian Al-Ghazali claimed that the promise of sexual pleasure 'was a powerful motivation to incite men... to adore God so as to reach heaven.' I think myself that such imagery may easily be misunderstood and the self-immolation of suicide bombers makes one aware that the promise of heavenly rewards may be misused for political purposes.

As for the wicked, the Qur'an says that they will burn 'as long as heaven and earth endure' (11, 106-7). There are two conditions attached to this. One is 'except as Allah wills' and the other, in the view of some theologians, is that the punishments are not eternal because the heavens and the earth as we see them are not eternal. Another verse says, 'Those who deny Our revelations, we will roast in a fire. As often as their skins are consumed. We will give them fresh skins, so that they may taste the torment.' (4, 56).

Imagery of heaven and hell is easily misleading, especially if taken too literally, as we are bound to use comparisons from this life which are not relevant to a life which we cannot imagine. The New Testament speaks of heavenly banquets and there are also grim warnings of hell 'where their worm dieth not and the fire is not quenched.' (Mark 9, 43-4 AV).

Both Christianity and Islam try to balance belief in both the justice and mercy of God. God's justice is important, although it is not perhaps given adequate attention in modern Christian circles. The justice of God emphasises moral responsibility:our behaviour matters. It also suggests that there is redress in another world to the injustices and suffering of this world. Yet too easily pictures of God's punishment of sinners can give a picture of a God of vengeance, which is especially dangerous when humans take it upon themselves to be agents of that vengeance. Umar ibn Khattab told of the occasion when some prisoners of war were brought to the Prophet. Among them was a woman who ran all over the place looking for her child. When she found it, she lifted it close toward her and suckled it. The Prophet then asked, 'Can you imagine this woman throwing her child into the fire?' When his companions said, 'No', Muhammad said, 'God is much more compassionate towards his servants than she is towards the child.'

The Qur'an suggests that those who appear before God after death are involved in deciding their own guilt or innocence. God will say to every person,

'Read thine (own) record:
Sufficient is thy soul
This day to make out
An account against thee' (17,14).

As the Saudi Arabian commentary says, 'Our true accusers are our own deeds.' The distinguished scholar Huston Smith explains,

'What death burns away is self-serving defences, forcing one to see with total objectivity how one has lived one's life. In the uncompromising light of that vision, where no dark and hidden corners are allowed, it is one's own actions that rise up to accuse or confirm.'

In St John's Gospel, Jesus says that he did not come to condemn the world. People condemn themselves by not coming to the light for fear that their deeds will be exposed (John 3, 17-20 and 12, 47-8).

In both religions there is the suggestion that in the presence of God, we shall gradually see our lives for what they are in the light of divine truth. Whether there is place for further repentance is not clear. As warners, neither Jesus nor Muhammad would have wanted to lessen the urgency of their call to repentance, yet both were deeply aware of divine mercy.

Sadly, the application of justice in some Islamic states does not reflect the compassion of God. As Farid Esack says, 'The idea of an Allah who is compassionate and merciful is one that we need to retrieve in order to recapture Islam from those who insist that our faith and Allah are only about anger and vengeance.' This is not to say that some so-called Christian countries are without fault. I find, for example, the continued use of capital punishment in the USA deeply disturbing.

The context in which Islam and Christianity influenced legal development was different. Unlike the early Muslims, the early Christians did not constitute a political entity or state, so they had no responsibility for framing or administering laws. Those who lived outside Palestine lived under the law of the Roman Empire, which was not based on revelation, but was roughly in accordance with the ethico-legal parts of the Mosaic law. When in the fourth century the Roman Empire accepted Christianity as the official religion, there was no need to create a new system of law based solely on the teaching of the Bible. Christians, therefore, generally accepted that it was possible to reach a satisfactory legal system based on sound reason apart from revelation. Thus in both mediaeval and modern Western Christendom, although the laws were expected to be in accordance with biblical teaching, it was not considered necessary to show how a particular law was derived from scriptural texts.

This over-lapping of civil law and personal and family law, which in some countries is reserved to religious courts, may be illustrated by the fact that when I officiate at a wedding as a clergyman of the Church of England, I not only bless the couple as a priest, but also act in a legal capacity in registering their marriage. In the twentieth century there has been increased questioning of Christian moral teaching and Britain has become a more multi-religious andn secularsociety. This has raised the question of the extent to which, subject to the law of the land, but religious communities in Britain should have their own legal systems for personal and family law.

Islam by contrast was a political unit from very early days - from Muhammad's Hijra to Medina. Even so, it did not have to construct a system of law out of nothing. In general the customs of the nomadic Arabs prevailed even in the towns of Mecca and Medina, although customary practices did not entirely fit urban life. Where something was unsatisfactory, the Qur'an gave new rules and tried to limit tribal vengeance and blood feuds, but otherwise the situation was unchanged.

As the Islamic state grew into an empire, influential Muslims came to think that the legal system should be based on the Qur'an, which, as we have already mentioned was to be interpreted in the light of the *hadith* or stories about the Prophet, as well as with analogy, precedent and the mind of the community. The great jurist al-Shafi'i (d. 820) produced a theory of 'the roots of law,' which gained wide acceptance. He showed how to interpret the Sunna (customary practice) and how to apply the rules of the Qur'an and the Sunna to new situations. In theory, therefore, it was possible to show how the whole legal system was derived from the God-given law, or *Shari'a,* revealed in the Qur'an. The legal system was therefore what is called theocratic - it was based on the revelation of God, whereas the law of Christendom was primarily based on sound reason and, especially in English Common Law, precedent.

Shari'a was intended for a Muslim society. Provision was made for non-Muslims who were known as Dhimmi. Originally intended for People of the Book - Jews, Christians and Zoroastrians - this status came to refer to all non-Muslims living in a Muslim state.

Many colonial powers imposed Western legal systems on their empires. Some Muslim countries have retained or revised these. Others have reintroduced Islamic or Shari'a law. As has been mentioned, there are various schools of Shari'a. In some countries, such as Saudi Arabia, the Shari'a is based on the teaching of the Wahhabiya movement, which is ultra-conservative and puritanical. The Wahhabiya movement rejects centuries of development in Islamic legal thinking and is strict in its ban on luxury and on the introduction of non-Muslim or *kafir* practices, which in effect cover much of the behaviour and life-style of modern Western societies. The movement also treats those Muslims who do not accept their teaching as heretics.

It is important, therefore, to recognise that cruel punishments such as stoning for adultery or amputation of a hand for theft, which are unacceptable to western opinion, are equally unacceptable to many Muslims. It is also helpful to remember that the Arab society in which Muhammad came to have political power was one of tribal rivalries. As Kenneth Cragg makes clear the bonds of blood and kin-relationship were transformed into a faith-based unity with a single worship and command. The Qur'an sought to limit private retaliation. Although it is still allowed this, it insisted that revenge, if exacted, must be strictly limited, and made clear that forgiveness or compounding for money were preferable

> O you who believe!
> *Al-Qisas* (the Law of Equality in punishment)
> Is prescribed to you in the case of murder:
> The free for the free, the slave for the slave, and the female for the female.
> But if the killer is forgiven by the brother (or the relatives) of the killed Against blood money, then adhering to it with fairness and payment of Blood-money to the heir should be made in fairness
> This is an alleviation and mercy from your Lord...
> And there is (a saving of) life for you
> In the Law of Equality in punishment,
> O men of understanding, that you may become the pious. (2, 178-9).

Legal systems, based on the Qur'an tend to give greater weight to the injured party or his or her relatives than does British law. Nonetheless cruel punishments, wherever they occur, need to be challenged both in the name of God and in defence of human rights. True religion should emphasise the justice and mercy of God and seek to have this mirrored in human society.

This takes us back to the question of repentance and forgiveness. Most offences against another human being are also offences against God. This means that repentance addressed to God is necessary as well as compensation to the injured party.

If compensation is made and the repentance is genuine, is punishment still required? Maybe acceptance of punishment is a sign of contrition. It is interesting to compare stories of how Muhammad and Jesus dealt with a woman who had committed adultery. Mahmoud Ayoub tells how a woman, who had committed this offence confessed to the Prophet, and asked that she be duly punished, which meant being stoned. The woman was pregnant. The Prophet told her to go away and wait until the baby was born. In due course, she returned with the child in her arms and again asked for punishment. The Prophet sent her away again to nurse the child until it was weaned. The mother returned again leading her child who had a piece of bread in his mouth. Had the woman not returned and simply repented, she would have escaped punishment. But since she wished her sin to be expiated, the Prophet ordered that she be stoned to death. Afterwards he prayed over her and gave her an honourable burial. Umar b. al-Khattab, who was to become the second caliph, protested that Muhammad had prayed over a woman who had committed adultery. Muhammad replied, 'But she had performed such a sincere act of repentance which, if it were divided among seventy inhabitants of Madina, it would suffice them. Is there anything nobler than her offering her life freely to God?'

St John's Gospel tells of a woman, caught in the act of adultery, who was brought to Jesus by some religious leaders who pointed out that the Law required her to be stoned. Jesus replied, 'That one of you who is faultless shall throw the first stone.' Gradually, one by one, the accusers went away. Jesus then turned to the woman and asked her, "Has no one condemned you?" "No", she replied. Jesus answered, "Nor do I condemn you. You may go; do not sin again."

Religious teaching focuses on the inner relation of the soul to God, which is known only to God. Legal systems have to focus on outward behaviour. Neglect of prayers out of laziness and apostasy are offences before God, but the law has to be satisfied by an outward show of repentance. God's verdict has to be left till the Day of Judgement. If punishment is carried out here on earth, the intention is to bring the recalcitrant person back to the community or to make him an example to others.

Where injury is caused to another person, the first requirement of the wrongdoer is that he should compensate the victim. The prophet, however, urged victims to offer forgiveness:

Let them forgive and overlook,
Do you not wish
That Allah should forgive you? (24, 22).

According to an early tradition, Muhammed advised, 'If anyone would like God to save him from the anxieties of the Day of Resurrection, he should grant a respite to one who is in straitened circumstances or remit his debt.' Aisha reported that the Prophet said, 'Avert the infliction of prescribed penalties on Muslims as much as you can, and let a man go if there is any way out, for it is better for a leader to make a mistake in forgiving than to make a mistake in punishing'.

Any religious tradition is complex and the outsider especially should avoid quoting one verse or example as definitive for a religion's teaching on a particular matter. It may be that in terms of Biblical texts and their guidance for behaviour today, Christians are more willing to set them in a historical context, but most Muslims also read the revealed teaching in the context of the agreed interpretation of the community. Both faith communities to my mind need constantly to review moral teaching and behaviour according to the highest ethical standards of the faith and rightly there should be criticism of any behaviour that devalues other human beings.

Religions' role in peace-building and reconciliation

Religions should have an important role in bringing the teaching of forgiveness to *bear* on situations of conflict, many of which are inflamed by long memories of cruelty and injustice. It was suggested at the time of the Millennium that Christians should apologise for the Crusades. The Churches, sadly, declined to make an official apology, although a few brave Christians went to the Middle East to do so. Acknowledgment of past wrong-doing is a step towards healing its continuing poison.

Faith communities have a particular opportunity to play a healing role during the process of peace-building. The most striking recent example is South Africa. Archbishop Desmond Tutu, who chaired the Truth and Reconciliation Commission, has said, 'We here in South Africa are a living example of how forgiveness may unite people'. The example was set by Nelson Mandela. When he was released after twenty-seven years in jail, he declared that his mission was to the victim and the victimiser. Our miracle' Tutu continued, almost certainly would not have happened without the willingness of people to forgive, exemplified spectacularly in the magnanimity of Nelson Mandela.' It was recognised that the evils of the apartheid era had to be faced. A general amnesty, which would have amounted to amnesia was rejected, but also the Nuremberg option of the victors putting the vanquished on trial. The participation of white South Africans in the new nation was essential to its economic development. A third option - a Truth and Reconciliation Commission - was agreed. This was not like the one in Chile which was behind closed doors and on condition that General Pinochet and other members of the military junta were given amnesty. South Africa's third way was 'the granting of amnesty to individuals in exchange for a full disclosure relating to the crime for which amnesty was being sought.'

There are many dimensions to forgiveness and these are increasingly being studied. Forgiveness is essentially a religious concept, although there are important differences of emphasis between religions. I agree with Desmond Tutu that 'Without Forgiveness there really is no future', which is the title of the final chapter of his book *No Future Without Forgiveness.* He recognises that a papering over the cracks is a cheap peace that is no peace. 'True reconciliation exposes the awfulness, the abuse, the pain, the degradation, the truth... People are not being asked to forget... Forgiveness means abandoning your right to pay back the perpetrator in his own coin, but it is a loss which liberates the victim.' He ends the book by saying, 'God wants to show that there is life after conflict and repression - that because of forgiveness, there is a future.

Where conflict is also a clash between members of different faiths, there is a responsibility on religious leaders to call for reconciliation. Indeed, wherever there is an abuse of human rights, injustice or violence, people of faith need to speak and act together, inspired by the teachings of their scriptures. Strikingly, one of first occasions in South Africa on which people of different faiths shared in reciting passages from their scriptures was in a prison cell. Members of different religions who had taken part in a protest against apartheid were arrested and locked up. They passed the time by reciting passages from the Bible, the Qur'an and the Hindu Vedas.

Chapter 8. THE WHOLE OF LIFE

Staying with a distinguished heart specialist, who was a Muslim, on a visit to Chicago - in preparation for a Parliament of the World's Religions - I was shown to my room which had the usual provision for a guest, but in addition there was a prayer mat. I was pleased to use this for my own prayers. It was a reminder also to me of the faithful Muslim's wish to remember God in everything he or she does and or says.

Secularisation

This of course is the hope of devout Christians, but some of them may be reluctant to make their religious practices public. This is in part because of the secularisation of Western society. Secular and Secularisation, strictly speaking, are neutral descriptive terms Secularism is used to refer to a movement that opposes religion or at least wishes to exclude religion from public life. For example, in Britain, some Christians have been told they cannot wear a cross at work and, in France, Muslim women are not allowed to wear a *hijab* (or head scarf). Most Muslims, however, as Ataullah Siddiqui points out, use 'Secularism' in a wider sense to include materialism, modernity and the secularisation of society. They perceive this as a corrupting influence on their society and blame the West for the damage that secularism causes. They also often see it as side-effect of imperialism. as an extended arm of secularisation.

Public religious observance appears to be more evident today in Muslim countries than in most Christian societies. In the film 'Salmon Fishing in the Yemen', when the lead character and his colleague arrive at the Emir's palace, all the locals are bowing during their evening prayer. He turned to his colleague saying, 'I don't think I know anyone in England who goes to church, do you?' Certainly there has been a decline of public religious observance in Britain over the last fifty years. For example, at school we had a holiday on Ascension Day and a half holiday on a Saints Day - although the St Andrew's day half holiday was usually deferred to coincide with the Varsity Rugby match! Now, in Britain, shops open not only on Good Friday but on every Sunday, except Easter Day. Rather than speak of Christmas, some cities in Britain have created a 'Winter Festival'. Even practising Christians tend to compartmentalise their lives. I notice that if I go to the Prayer room at an airport, the other people there are usually Muslims. Even so, a recent survey in Britain suggests that 58% of the population still claim to be Christians and 15% go to church at least once a month. Atheists and Agnostics represent 33% of the population and are still in the minority.

Formal prayer (*salat*) is the second of the 'Pillars of the Faith' or 'Five Pillars of Islam.' Muslims publicly affirm their faith in the regular prayers which are offered five times a day. When I travelled once on Kuwait Airlines, as the flight began, a verse was read from the Qur'an. Royal Jordanian Airlines regularly indicate the direction of the Ka'bah at Mecca.

There are many reasons for the secularisation of Western society and the loss of the privileged position that Christianity once enjoyed. It allows for personal freedom, including freedom of speech, shown for example in the defence of Salman Rushdie's right to say what he wanted in his novel, *The Satanic Verses,* even though many Muslims thought that ridiculing religious beliefs should not be granted such freedom. By contrast laws to defend Islam in Pakistan have led to attacks on Christians merely for possessing Gospels. What are the limits to freedom of speech and when do those limits become oppressive?

In Islam, God's concern is for the whole of life. I have a little book called *Radiant Prayers.* It is a popular Muslim book of 'easy prayers'. There are prayers for every occasion - when the sun rises, on taking a bath, while looking into a mirror, on setting out on or returning from a journey. This may not seem strange to a devout Christian, it certainly is so to the modern secularist.

Yet soon after writing the above, I came across the following passage in Farid Esack's book *On Being a Muslim:*

'Our lives as Muslims are largely devoid of an ongoing and living connection with Allah. We confine this relationship to moments of personal difficulty; have it mediated through a professional class of religious figures - the managers of the sacred - or the formal rituals of the five daily prayers, the pilgrimage to Mecca and fasting in the month of Ramadan. Absent is the warmth evident from the following *hadith qudsi* (saying of Allah, in the words of the Prophet):

"When a servant of Mine seeks to approach Me through that which I like out of what I have made obligatory upon him (her) and continues to advance towards Me through voluntary effort beyond the prescribed, then I begin to love him (her). When I love him (her) I become the ears by which (s)he hears, the eyes by which (s)he sees, and the hands by which (s)he grasps, and the feet with which (s)he walks. When (s)he asks Me, I bestow upon him(her) and when (s)he seeks My protection, I protect him(her).'

This passage made me realise how difficult it is to understand the dynamic of a religion from outside. One can give an account of the teaching, but this may be an idealised version and not correspond to the actuality. Perhaps both Christians and Muslims and indeed members of other religions have the same struggle to be aware of the presence of God in everyday life. We have our various rituals - but none of us can judge the meaning another person attaches to them. Are they repeated by rote or are they a renewed encounter with God? As Farid Esack observes later in his book,

> 'It is... possible to complete all one's legal obligations in respect of the prayers and bypass Allah completely... "This in the presence of Allah" is a vital element in prayer that many of us seem to have sacrificed at the altar of legality. We are able to rush through the "whole thing" in a few minutes flat to get it over with."

This question of attention in worship is nothing new, although it may be highlighted by the complexity of modern society, especially where the assumptions of shared belief no longer exist. Esack himself says that 'We have never been as alienated from ourselves, from others and from Allah as in this age.' Later, he comments that 'Accumulation, the sister of consumerism, has impoverished us spiritually and humanly.'

Muslims and Christians face the same challenges in an increasingly alien society and differences are probably more to do with societies' varied historical-social situations in than disagreements about religious teaching.

There are, however, perhaps differences of emphasis on wealth-creation and sexual enjoyment between the two religions. There is little evidence of the ascetic or world-renouncing attitude to found in some forms of Christianity, although, as we shall see, Muslims are required to fast during the hours of daylight for the month of Ramadan and I have found the positive attitudes of Islam helpful in my own thinking.

Wealth

Al Faruqi, in his book Islam, wrote, 'Every Muslim desires and plans to become a "millionaire" if he or she takes Islam seriously.' He insists that the money should be earned and not accumulated by cheating or exploitation of natural resources. Further, Muslims should provide for the poor by paying *Zakat*, which is the Third Pillar of Islam, and by other charitable giving. *Zakat* prescribes that two and one-half percent of a Muslim's total wealth should be distributed to the needy, 'Muslims believe that God commands them to produce wealth, so that all may live and prosper. They thank God if their efforts succeed, and they bear it patiently if they fail.'

In the teaching of Jesus, however, there is a suspicion of riches. Jesus told various parables warning against the dangers of wealth and he said that 'You cannot serve God and Money' (Matthew 6, 24). When he was approached by a member of the ruling class who asked what he should do to win eternal life, Jesus said to him, 'Sell everything you have and distribute to the poor, and you will have riches in heaven'(Luke 18, 22). St Francis' renunciation of wealth has been copied by many monks and nuns who have taken vows of poverty, chastity and obedience.

Sexuality

Celibacy, which the Roman Catholic Church requires of all priests, is not regarded as a virtue in Islam. In Al Faruqi's words:

> 'For Muslims sex is as natural as food and drink, growth and death. It is God created, God blessed, God instituted. It is not laden with guilt, but, is innocent. Indeed, sex is highly desirable. The Qur'an prohibits celibacy for the sake of God. The Prophet ennobled marriage by making it his *sunnah*, or example, and hence the norm for every Muslim male and female. Like everything else pertinent to life on earth, Islam made sexual gratification of men and women a thing of piety, virtue and felicity.'

As has been already mentioned, there is no doctrine of original sin in Islam. The Baptism service in The Church of England's *Book of Common Prayer* (now seldom used,) begins, 'Forasmuch as all men are conceived and born in sin.' According to St Augustine, Adam's original sin has been transmitted from parent to child ever since through 'concupiscence' or the sinful sexual excitement which accompanies procreation. The Qur'an's account of Adam and Eve's disobedience is

85

not linked to human sexuality. 'Islam regards sex', says Faruqi, 'as an innocent good and the pursuit of knowledge as a paramount duty, not as evil.'

Christian attitudes to human sexuality have been far more ambiguous. Jesus, tradition holds, was unmarried, as was St Paul. Influenced in part by Hellenistic thinking, which thought of physical pleasure as ensnaring the soul, many monks and nuns chose celibacy. Although many Christian thinkers would now repudiate Augustine's teaching about original sin and take a far more positive and Biblical view of sexuality, certainly in the past guilt feelings have been quite common among Christians.

Paradoxically, past inhibitions in the West have today been replaced by what most Muslims and many Christians would regard as undue permissiveness. On the other hand, Christians are shocked by stories of honour killings or, in some part of the Muslim world, the stoning of women caught in adultery.

Western society seems to be obsessed by sex. One of the attractions of Islam for some western converts - many of whom are drawn to the faith by Sufism - is its clear moral teaching. This is especially so for women converts as well as for so-called 'reverts' or nominal Muslims who become committed to the practice of the faith. Jemima Goldsmith, writing in *The Times*, insisted that she converted 'of her own conviction.' She said that 'it would seem that a Western woman's happiness hinges largely on her access to night-clubs, alcohol and revealing clothes, although such superficialities have very little to do with true happiness.' The *Times,* in an editorial in November 1993, drew attention to the growing number of women in Britain and the USA who were positively attracted by the sense of sisterhood and community which they discovered in Islam. Nouria, who converted after finding some verses of the Qur'an in a dustbin, emphasised the sisterhood.

> 'There is no such thing as a Muslim woman on her own nor a single Muslim parent on her own. If anyone with a commitment to Islam sees you in *hijab* (the scarf) and you're suffering, they step in and help. That's abnormal in Britain.'

Female converts claim that in Islam they already have the equal status that the feminist movement is striving for. They keep their own name in marriage and they also retain anything they inherit and whatever they earn - a right Muslim women have had for 1,400 years! They complain that Western emancipation means copying men, whereas Islam recognises separate spheres.

The Veil

Does traditional dress enhance the dignity of Muslim women or is it a sign of male dominance? This is a question which is heatedly debated in the Muslim world and also sometimes seen as divisive in secular multi-religious society.

Some Muslim women strongly object to the veil. There is clearly a public feeling that the veil and even more the *birqa* are a sign that women are treated as 'second-class' in Muslim society and this, of course, offends feminists, including some Muslim women The South African Muslim Farid Esack told me that when he visited Uzbekistan in 1988, - when it was still part of the Soviet Union – his guide said to him, 'You will be delighted to know how alive Islam is; you will not see a single woman on our streets.'

Others Muslim women, see wearing the veil, is a rejection of the sexual promiscuity of British society, of which many Christians are critical. Hudda Khattub, who wrote the *Muslim Woman's Handbook*, said, 'Muslims don't keep shifting their goal posts. Christianity changes, like the way some people have said pre-marital sex is Ok if it's with person you are going to marry. It seems so wishy-washy. Islam was constant about sex and about praying five times a day.' A Muslim man, who has returned to the practice of his faith, said his whole attitude to women had changed. 'When I meet a Muslim woman nowadays with full *hajib*, covered up I can talk to her, really communicate – it's no longer about sex.' Other Muslims say they have 'equality of status' whereas Western women's equality seems to be about imitating men.

Muslims are often critical of Western permissiveness. Huda Khattub wrote in *The Muslim Woman's Handbook*:

'Muslims don't keep shifting their goal posts' Christianity changes, like the way some have said pre-marital sex is OK if it's with the person you're going to marry. It seems so wishy-washy. Islam was constant about sex and about praying five times a day.'

Islam, in Faruqi's words, 'vehemently' condemns sexual promiscuity because it is by definition a violation of responsibility of one or the other party. Marriage in Islam is not a sacrament but a civil contract. Although the Qur'an allows a man to have up to four wives, this is on condition that each is treated equally. Some Muslim scholars, such as Ameer Ali in *The Spirit of Islam* says that this is emotionally impossible and that, therefore, monogamy is ideal. It is often recognised that at the time of the Prophet many women were widows and the preponderance of women in the population encouraged polygamy.

Perhaps the church should have been more critical of changing norms. Yet, if many Western Christians are too accepting of the permissive society, some Muslim regimes are very harsh in enforcing traditional morality. I felt distinctly uneasy when in a recent TV documentary some Muslim women agreed that adultery should be a capital offence. The Qur'an itself is severe in the punishment of adultery, saying that both the man and the woman should be beaten with a hundred lashes 'without any feeling of pity.' (24, 2.) Women who are guilty of immorality are to be confined to their homes until they die - but those who bring false accusations are also severely punished

In any case, such comparisons are unfruitful. Neither religion has much to boast about in its treatment of women and both religions have been male-dominated. Rather than argue over the past, theologians in both religions need radically to rethink traditional teaching and interpretation of the texts.

Farid Esack claims that 'reading a text through the eyes of the marginalised who yearn for justice would yield a meaning in harmony with what Allah, the Just, desires for all humankind.' Several Muslim women scholars, such as Fatima Mernissi or Riffat Hassan, are shaping a new reading of the Qur'an and the *Hadith*. Muhammad himself revolutionised the status of women. He stamped out female infanticide, accepted the evidence of women and allowed women to inherit. He washed and stitched his own clothes and shared the cooking chores with his wife. Islamic law, however, Esack says, has failed to keep up with human progress in the area of gender justice. 'We have betrayed the prophetic intention of justice and equality for all Allah's people.'

I would be equally critical of much in the Christian tradition and in a chapter in *Abraham's Children*, on 'Gender in Christianity', I quoted Linda Woodhead who has said that 'what is needed is fresh and creative reflection on the mystery of human sexual difference which is as responsibly related to the Christian tradition as it is to contemporary concerns.'

Homosexuality

The 'Declaration Toward a Global Ethic' spoke about gender equality, but not about equality for people whatever their sexual orientation. Both the Bible (Leviticus 8, 22 and 20, 13 and Romans 1, 26-27) and the Qur'an (15, 73f and 26, 165f) are usually read as condemning homosexuality. Churches in the West are divided on their attitudes to homosexuality, especially whether priests and bishops can be openly 'gay.' In most of the Muslim world any public expression of homosexuality is strongly condemned and may be severely punished.

Homosexuality is also severely punished - in some countries by death. *Al-Fatiha*, an American based 'international organisation for lesbian, gay, bisexual and transgender Muslims' estimates that 4,000 homosexuals have been executed in Iran since the 1979 revolution. Large scale public executions of homosexuals have also been carried out by the Taliban in Afghanistan. Elsewhere, as an article in *The Economist* said, 'Gay life in the open in Muslim-majority countries is rare, but, the closet is spacious.'

What is acceptable or unacceptable in terms of sexual behaviour differs sharply in modern and more traditional societies. People seem to live in different historical time zones. The bigger question for both Christians and Muslims is to what extent traditional understandings of scripture are to be modified in the light of new understandings of human sexuality and changing patterns of socail life. ,

For example, in Western society people's expectations of marriage have often increased. Contraception and financial independence have given women greater freedom. In many democratic societies it is thought that the state has no business to interfere in a person's personal life style, unless it is harmful to others. Modern studies also suggest that homosexuality is genetically caused rather than a personal matter of choice. This view, however, is rejected by many Muslim leaders. Dr Muzammil Siddiqi of the Islamic Society of North America is quoted as saying, 'Homosexuality is a moral disorder. It is a moral disease, a sin and corruption... No person is born homosexual, just like no one is born a liar or a murderer. 'There are, however, Muslim organisations which are trying to encourage a more sympathetic approach. *Al-Fatiha*, for example, seeks to work with the progressive wing of Islam 'to enlighten the world that Islam is a religion of tolerance and not hate, and that Allah (God) loves His creation, no matter what their sexual orientation might be.' Arash Naraghi, an Iranian academic in America, has suggested that the verses which condemn homosexuality, like those on slavery, stem from common beliefs at the time of writing and should now be re-examined. Sheikh Muhammad Hussein Fadlallah, the late spiritual leader of Hizbullah in the Lebanon, has conceded that more research is needed to understand homosexuality.

Multi-Culturalism or Britishness?

Questions raised by the Veil, like those discussed by the Archbishop of Canterbury in his lecture on *Shari'a* and British Law are complex and important. They point to other even more essential questions. 'How do we strike the right balance between allowing faith communities a proper freedom and affirming our shared life together?' If some of the differences in a few immigrants' way of life appear to the majority to be immoral – such as suttee or female circumcision or forced marriages - the question is more complicated

'What should be the balance between multi-culturalism and social cohesion or Britishness? My ideal would be that of the Chief Rabbi – namely - 'a community of communities.' This requires respect for the beliefs and practices of particular faith communities, as for many people religion is bound up with their sense of identity - what they may eat, what they should wear, whom they should not marry. At the same time, if society is not to become fragmented, there needs to be a recognition of the values that we share and which provide the basis for the society to which we all belong.

I welcome maximum freedom for all faith communities in Britain within the context of universal moral law and British law. And British law continues to adapt itself. Many changes have taken place in my lifetime. People can take the oath in court on any of the world scriptures. Most schools offer a vegetarian option. Firms should allow workers time to observe holy days, including Good Friday. There are Jewish and Muslim as well as Christian faith schools. There is now provision for 'Special Guardianship' of children, as Muslims do not agree with the adoption of children.

I think there should be further accommodation of Muslim concerns. For example, as you know a marriage in church is both a religious and legal occasion. If a couple get married in a mosque, they are required also to have a civil marriage at the registry office. Provided that the British law that marriage is intended to be life-long and monogamous is affirmed, I see no reason why both a religious and civil marriage should not be held at a Mosque.

90

On so many matters, the underlying question is how does one read scripture? Should one compare what the scriptures say and so talk about an idealised situation which has little reality - or compare actual situations which may have been historically and socially conditioned.

At the Parliament of Religions in Chicago in 1993, members of the Assembly, including leading Muslims and Christians, in the 'Declaration Toward a Global Ethic' committed themselves to work for an equal partnership between men and women. Men and women were urged to respect each other. At the same time sexual exploitation was denounced. There is some debate whether equal partnership means 'equality' or 'equity'. Do the physical differences of men and women lead to some differences in role, although not in respect or worth?

There is also the question - still too little discussed - about the use of inclusive religious language and allowing women a full and equal role in the life of a faith community. Christian talk of God as 'Father, Son and Holy Spirit' and the repeated references to God as Father is very masculine - the Holy Spirit is normally spoken of as male. Allah, although beyond all attributes, is assumed to be male in translations of the Qur'an. In some Christian churches - but still a minority - women may now be priests or ministers. In 1994 Professor Amina Wadud spoke at the Claremont Main Road Mosque in Cape Town. The *Cape Times* - inaccurately in fact - described her as 'the first woman ever to do so in South Africa.' At the same time, women congregants at the mosque came down from upstairs to pray alongside the males, with a rope separating them. There are similar developments, although very rare, in a few Muslim communities in Western Europe or North America.

There is debate and division in the Muslim world, but beside the 'Pillars of Islam' already mentioned the two other pillars - *Ramadan* or the month of Fasting and the *Hajj* or Pilgrimage to Mecca reinforce the unifying sense of belonging to the *umma* or community of faith.

Ramadan.

Fasting (*Sawm*) is obligatory for Muslims during the month of Ramadan. It is also practised to compensate for days missed during Ramadan - for example, on a journey, or because of illness or pregnancy or while breast feeding - and in fulfilment of a personal vow or as a pious act. Fasting should be preceded by the intention; but there is a saying that 'if one made a pilgrimage for God and his

Prophet it would be rewarded, but not if the intention was to gain a wife.' Al-Ghazali emphasised that the real purpose of fasting was 'to purify the heart and so concentrate all its intention upon God.' Some contemporary writers also highlight the importance of Ramadan as an act of solidarity with the millions of people who do not have the basic necessities of life.

Ramadan is observed in the ninth month of the Islamic year and is a blessed month 'in which the Qur'an was revealed, a guidance for mankind and clear proofs for the guidance .. So whoever sees the crescent of the moon, must fast for a month. Whoever is ill or on a journey, the same number of days that were not observed must be made up from other days. Allah intends for your ease and does not want to make things difficult for you.' (2, 185)

During Ramadan adults should abstain from food, drink, smoking and sexual relations during daylight hours, which are estimated as beginning 'when the white thread becomes distinct to you from the black thread at dawn.' (2, 187) People are advised to have a good meal just before dawn and to break the fast with water or dates and then have a large meal, which may become a festive family occasion.

Ramadan is also a time of greater prayer and devotion. The 27th night Laylat al-Qadr (the 'Night of Power') is the holiest of the year.(97, 3). The fast ends with the feast of Id al-Fitr.

Many Muslims are strict in their observance of Ramadan. When our daughter had an *au pair* girl from Turkey, her parents telephoned her every day to tell her the exact time that the fast would begin. To outsiders, Ramadan seems very demanding, but Muslims often say that it is indeed a time of renewal.

Christians in the Middle Ages fasted regularly, but after the Reformation, Protestants mostly abandoned the practice, although there is some renewed interest today.

Hajj

'Pilgrimage to the house of Allah is a duty unto Allah for mankind, for him who can find a way thither.' Over the centuries the faithful have made great sacrifices and long arduous journeys to reach their goal 'on foot and on every lean camel.' (Qur'an 22, 27). Now, with benefit of flights available from many parts of the world during the Hajj, alone, 2-3 million people visit Makkah. Millions also visit during Ramadan, at other times of religious significance, and during school holidays.

The prescribed ceremonies are detailed in the *hadith* - stories about the Prophet and are based on his Farewell Pilgrimage. The area around Mecca is designated as holy, so men and women wear special white clothes and keep themselves in a state of purity.

In Mecca, the pilgrimage includes visiting the Masjid al-Haram - the mosque at Mecca; walking seven times round the Ka'ba, which is about 35 feet by 40 feet and 50 feet high and is said to be the house that Adam built and that was rebuilt by Ibrahim (Abraham) and his son. If possible pilgrims kiss the Black Stone - said to be of meteoric origin - which is embedded in the Ka'ba. On the eighth day, pilgrims move on eastwards to Mina or to Arafat where it is said that Adam and Eve, who fled separately from the Garden of Eden met again. Later pilgrims return to Mecca and some also visit Medina.

All these rituals, of course, are given a spiritual meaning. As the Qur'an says, people come 'that they may witness things that are of benefit to them in the hereafter and also of some value to them in this world.'(Qur'an 22, 28). As the beautiful Saudi book *Pilgrimage to Mecca* asks, 'What is the underlying reason for kissing the Black Stone if it is not the pledge of alleigance and fidelity to God?'

Besides the personal benefit the *Hajj* binds the faithful together. 'High on the list of benefits,' says the beautiful Saudi book *Pilgrimage to Mecca*, 'is the gathering of Muslims from all over the world at a single time in a single place with among them the influential figures of Islamic countries, so that they may get to know each other and avail themselves of this blessed opportunity to discuss the issues of the Muslim world. And no one but Allah conveneth such a solemn assembly.'

A non-Muslim is not allowed to journey to Mecca, but pictures, exhibitions, videos and books convey something to the spiritual significance of the *Hajj* to those who have taken part. Best of all is to let those who have made the Hajj tell you what it has meant to them

For many Christians, a pilgrimage to the Holy Land is a high point of their spiritual journey. If not on earth, will Muslims and Christians in the next world find their destination is the same? As John Hick wrote in *God and the Universe of Faiths*, 'In St John's vision of the heavenly city at the end of the Christian scriptures (Revelation 21, 22) it is said that there is no temple - no Christian church or chapel, no Jewish synagogue, no Hindu or Buddhist temple, no Muslim mosque, no Sikh gurdwara... For all these exist in time, as ways through time to eternity.' In the heavenly city, The Lord God Almighty is the temple and the glory of God gives its light to all peoples (Revelation, 21, 22-24).

Chapter. 10 SAINTS AND SCHOLARS

If many Christians are ignorant of or misunderstand the Qur'an and its messenger, the Prophet Muhammad, they have even less awareness of the rich contribution that the world of Islam has made to many aspects of civilization. Here there is room only to provide a glimpse of a few outstanding saints and scholars.

Rabia

Rabia al-Adawiyah, who was born in about 713, transformed the early asceticism of Islam into a mysticism of love. She was the fourth child - Rabia means 'fourth' – of poor parents. She was abducted at an early age and sold into slavery. Eventually, her master who had watched her devoutly at prayer, set her free.

After a time in the desert, Rabia came back and, living in a small cell, devoted herself to worship. She began to attract followers and also offers of marriage, which she declined. She had many offers of marriage but refused them all. She lived a long life of simplicity and prayer.

Islamic mysticism or Sufism (*Tasawwuf*) now has an influence well beyond the Muslim world. The word Sufi, originally indicated the woollen garment worn by early Muslim ascetics. Other terms for these holy people are 'fakir' and 'dervish' meaning 'the poor'.

The mystics' desire was for direct personal experience of God's love and full union with the Divine. Although the Prophet Muhammad was not an ascetic some pious people in reaction to the worldliness of the early Umayyad period (661-749 CE) chose a life of celibacy, poverty and asceticism. They withdrew from the world, which they deemed 'a hut of sorrows' to weep for their sins.

Rabia changed this ascetic movement into a mysticism of love. Although she was afraid of God's rejection, she insisted that neither fear nor hope was the reason for her devotion, as these prayers show:

> *O my Lord, if I worship Thee from fear of Hell, burn me in Hell,*
> *And if I worship Thee from hope of Paradise, exclude me thence;*
> *But if I worship Thee for Thine own sake*
> *Then withhold not from me Thine Eternal Beauty.*

or

O my Lord, whatever share of this world Thou dost bestow on me,
bestow it on Thine enemies
and whatever share of the next world Thou dost give me,
give it to Thy friends.
Thou art enough for me.'

There is a famous story of Rabia that one day she was seen by a number of holy people with fire in one hand and water in the other. 'What are you doing?' she was asked. 'I am going to light a fire in Paradise and to pour water on Hell so that both veils (i.e. hindrances to the true vision of God) may completely disappear from the pilgrims and their purpose may be sure and the servants of God may see Him, without any object of hope or motive of fear.'

Interestingly an engraving of this scene has been found in a work, published in 1644, called *Caritee* by the French Quietist Camus. Rabia is not named in the book, but stories of her had been brought to France by Joinville, who was chancellor to King Louis IX of France.

Rabia lived to be nearly ninety. As she felt death was near, she asked to be alone 'to leave the way free for the messengers of God Most High.' From outside, her friends heard a voice saying, 'O soul at rest, return to thy Lord, satisfied with Him, giving satisfaction to Him. So enter among my servants and enter into my Paradise.'

Rabia had a decisive influence on the development of Sufism and was quoted by almost all the great Sufi teachers. The Sufi aim is by overcoming the self, or ego, to attain union with God. Although that union in all its fullness is only possible after death, it can in part be experienced in anticipation in this life. By following the Sufi mystic path, the seeker for God grows in penitence, patience, gratitude, hope, holy fear, voluntary poverty, asceticism, complete dependence upon God and finally love.

Rabia was by no means the only Muslim woman saint. The Prophet himself said, 'Paradise lies at the feet of mothers.' The influence of some women on the development of Islam and especially the Sufis and also the Sufi emphasis on love needs to be better known. It would help to correct the often one-sided view of Islam prevalent in the Western world. As Rabia said, love for God leaves no place for any enemies.

Al-Ghazali

Al-Ghazali, who was himself influenced by Rabia is considered the greatest Muslim religious authority after the Prophet Muhammad. He has deeply influenced Islamic jurisprudence, theology, philosophy and mysticism, but perhaps his greatest achievement was to integrate the Sufi mysticism, of which many orthodox thinkers were suspicious and highly critical, into mainstream theological thought.

Abu Hamid Muhammad, better known as al-Ghazali (his name is sometimes spelt al-Ghazzali) was born in 1058 CE, in the North East of the Old Persian Empire at Tus (near Mashad in present day Iran). Tus was at that time a centre of scholarship and it was also the birthplace of the Persian poet Omar Khayyam (1048-1125), who was an older contemporary of al-Ghazali.

Clearly al-Ghazali was a very bright student and maybe over-eager and ambitious. Later in life he wrote that a student should not pester a teacher when he is tired, nor, after the class, follow him, asking questions. He also said that a boy's bed should be hard and that he should take plenty of exercise and after school he should have time to enjoy himself. 'All work and no play', he wrote, 'will deaden a boy's heart and spoil his intelligence and make life grievous unto him.'

His academic brilliance led the Vizier to appoint him, at the early age of 34, to the chair of theology in Baghdad. His soul, however, was not satisfied. His study of Sufism made him aware that no amount of knowledge is a substitute for experience.

'It became clear to me that what is most distinctive of mysticism is something which cannot be apprehended by study, but only by immediate experience (*dhawq* – literally tasting), by ecstasy and by a moral change. What a difference there is between *knowing* the definition of health and satiety... and *being* healthy and satisfied. I apprehended clearly that the mystics were men who had real experiences, not men of words and that I had already progressed as far as was possible by way of intellectual apprehension.'

He struggled for six months between desire to follow the Sufi way and a reluctance to abandon his position and his family. Then God intervened and he found himself unable to lecture – 'my tongue would not utter a single word.' So he made provision for his family, then left home to seek seclusion in Damascus. Subsequently he journeyed to Jerusalem, spending long hours in the beautiful Dome of the Rock and then to Mecca.

Eventually, as he said, 'the entreaties of my children drew me back to my home country.' Living quietly in the city where he had studied he wrote his major work, *Ihya 'ulum al-din* ('The Revival of Religious Sciences') and other important books. Then in 1106, he returned for a time to lecture at Baghdad, but only in obedience to God, not from personal ambition. In due course he retired again and died at the age of fifty-three.

It is said that on the day of his death, after his ablutions, al-Ghazali asked for his shroud. He then took it, kissed it and laid it over his eyes, saying, 'Most gladly do I enter into the Presence of the King.' One story says that when he knew death was approaching, he asked to be left alone. Next morning when his friends entered they found a beautiful poem beside his still body:

> *Say to my friends, when they look upon me, dead,*
> *Weeping for me and mourning me in sorrow*
> *Do not believe that this body you see is myself.*
> *In the name of God, I tell you, it is not I ...*
> *I am a pearl, which has left its shell deserted,*
> *It was my prison, where I spent my time in grief.*
> *I am a bird, and this body was my cage*
> *Whence I have now flown forth and it is left as a token,*
> *Praise be to God, Who hath now set me free ...*
> *Think not that death is death, nay, it is life,*
> *A life that surpasses all we could dream of here,*
> *While in this world ...*
> *Think of the mercy and love of your Lord,*
> *Give thanks for His grace and come without fear ...*
> *I give you now a message of good cheer*
> *May God's peace and joy for evermore be yours.*

Despite his intellectual brilliance al-Ghazali recognised that union with God cannot be achieved by study. The ordinary person's devotion is as important as the scholar's learning. 'Trust the religion of the old women', he said at the end of his life. 'Such experience, if genuine, results in a transformed life.'

The influences upon Al-Ghazali and his influence on others is a reminder that spiritual wisdom does not recognise national or religious barriers. Al-Ghazali studied extensively and travelled widely. He, therefore, drew on a great range of learning and experience. He was influenced by Plotinus (c.250-270 CE) and Neo-

Platonism. Of course, he often referred to the Qur'an and the traditions about the Prophet and to Muslim scholars such as Avicenna (980-1087). He was probably acquainted with the Old Testament and some Jewish writers as well as with the New Testament, which was available in Arabic. He quotes from Mark's Gospel and from Jesus himself. For example he compares religious teachers to shepherds who protect their sheep from the wolf and in asking what use is salt if it has lost its savour. In speaking of Christ, he held Christians were wrong to think of him as one with God. It was like those who suppose that the reflection in a mirror is the object itself. Christians, Al-Ghazali wrote, beheld the radiance of God's light shining in Jesus, but were mistaken in thinking the Divine nature could be one with human nature. Nonetheless he acknowledged what was true in other people's beliefs, even if he pointed out where their teaching differed from the Qur'an.

Just as Al-Ghazali was influenced by others, so he influenced not only later Sufi writers, but also Jewish scholars such as Maimonides and perhaps the Zohar, which is the central text of Kabbalah – the Jewish mystical tradition. The great Christian scholar St Thomas Aquinas (1225-1274) studied Arabic writers and acknowledged his indebtedness to them. The poet Dante (1265-1321), who wrote of the Beatific Vision, quoted Al-Ghazali as one of his sources and the French mystic Blaise Pascal (1623-1662) knew of his writings and like Al-Ghazali held that truth can only be reached by love.

Avicenna and Averroes

Avicenna and Averroes, like al Ghazali influenced Christian thinkers and played a vital part in transmitting the works of the Greek philosophers Plato and Aristotle to the Christian West.

Avicenna, as Ibn Sina (980-1037) is known in the West, was born near Bukhara, now in Uzbekistan. Arab Muslim armies had come to the area in the late seventh and early eighth centuries, but the population was a mixture of Zoroastrians, Buddhists and some Christians and Jews.

Avicenna was a precocious child with an amazing memory. By the age of ten, he knew the Qur'an and many poems by heart. Avicenna was sent to a local greengrocer to learn the new 'Arabic' arithmetic, with its distinctive use of the zero, which was replacing the Persian system of finger calculation. He was also taught Islamic law, according to the liberal Hanafi tradition, by a noted jurist in the town. A resident tutor was employed to teach him philosophy, which included the study of Aristotle and Euclid. Avicenna then turned to medicine and the study of Galen, the second-century Greek physician.

By the age of sixteen, Avicenna was practising medicine and discovering new cures. His reputation was made when he successfully cured a Samanid prince. As a reward, Avicenna was given access to the royal library. In an age of manuscript literature, when books were rare and prized possessions, one can imagine his delight. 'I saw', he later wrote, 'books whose very titles are unknown to many, and which I never saw before or since.' When he came upon a new book, Avicenna went at once to the hardest passages to judge the author's scholarship rather than wasting time on the repetition of material with which he was already familiar.

In contrast to al-Ghazali, Avicenna believed it was possible to provide a philosophical basis for faith. Influenced by Plotinus (c.205-70), Avicenna held that God is the necessary existent. Avicenna's works were translated into Latin and had considerable influence on Mediaeval Christian theologians, such as St Thomas. Aquinas. 'The great insight of Avicenna as a philosopher' in the words of L.E Goodman, 'was the recognition of the compatibility of contingency, by which Islamic thinkers tried to canonise the scriptural idea of creation, and the metaphysics of necessity, in which the followers of Aristotle had enshrined the idea that the goal of science is understanding why and how things must be as they are.'

Study of Avicenna's philosophy, however, was banned for a time in the thirteenth century, but again permitted by Pope Gregory IX in 1231. Although he was given the honorific title of *ash-Shaykh ar-Ra'is* or 'The Leading Wise Man', his philosophical writings have been criticised by a number of orthodox Muslim theologians in the past.

The same was true of the last of the great Islamic philosophers Averroes or Ibn Rushd (1126-198) who was born in Spain nearly a century after Avicenna's death, at a time of political struggle between Almoravids and the Almohads and also of theological tension between the more open approach popular at Seville and the strict orthodoxy at Cordova (Cordoba).

His scholarship came to the attention of Ibn Tufayl (d. 1185), the leading philosopher of the period and court physician to the Caliph. In 1169 Averroes was introduced to the Caliph Abu Ya 'qub Yusuf by Ibn Tufayl. According to Averroes' own account of the meeting, 'the Prince asked me, "What is their (the philosophers') opinion about the heavens – Are they eternal or created?" Confusion and fear took hold of me, and I began to make excuses and deny that I had ever concerned myself with philosophical learning... The Prince of Believers (i.e. The Caliph) understood my fear and confusion ... and set me at ease until I spoke. He then learned how competent I was in that subject. When I withdrew he ordered for me a gift of money, a magnificent robe of honour and a steed.'

The Caliph also wanted understandable summaries of Aristotle's writings.' and for twenty five years Averroes devoted his energies to writing commentaries on and summaries of most of Aristotle's works. These clearly presented commentaries are included in the Latin version of Aristotle's complete works and they exerted considerable influence on subsequent Christian and Jewish thinkers. Indeed Averroes became known in the Christian world as 'The Commentator.'

Soon after the decisive meeting with the Caliph, Averroes was appointed the religious judge of Seville and soon afterwards chief judge of Cordova. Then in 1182 he became physician royal at the court of the Almohad dynasty, at Marrakesh in Morocco. But in 1195, the new Caliph, yielding to public pressure, ordered Averroes' books to be burned, accusing him of heresy and irreligion. The teaching of philosophy and science was banned –except for astronomy, medicine and administration. On one occasion Averroes was driven from the mosque in Cordova by an angry crowd of worshippers. Averroes was hurt by this and by the reputation that he had acquired of being a bad Muslim. Averroes himself was exiled to Lucena, which is South East of Cordova. Averroes was quickly restored to favour, but died soon after these traumatic events at the age of seventy- two.

Still today in Islam and indeed other religions creative thinkers are viewed with suspicion. In the words of Oliver Leaman, 'Averroes' reputation within the Islamic community did not remain high after his death and there is little evidence that he influenced the development of thought within Islam until quite recently. He had a far more successful after life among the Jewish communities in the medieval world and a widespread effect upon the Christian world.' Now as some Muslim scholars seeks to relate Islam constructively to the modern world, there is renewed interest in Avicenna and Averroes.

Ibn 'Arabi and Jalal-ad-Din ar-Rumi

Sufism, certainly, is widely influential today well beyond the world of Islam. If you type the name 'Rumi' into Google you get over a quarter of a million items.

Ibn 'Arabi (b. 1165- 1240) although not so well known as Rumi has been called The 'Revivifier of Religion.'

He was born in Murcia, which is in Andalusia in Southern Spain. In his early teens, he was overcome by a spiritual call that quickly led to a vision of God. He said that everything that he subsequently said and wrote was 'the differentiation of the universal reality comprised by that look.' During that early period, he had a number of visions of Jesus, whom he called his first guide on the path to God. It seems he did not enter formal Sufi training until he was nineteen and it was not until he was thirty that he left Spain for the first time. In 1200, he had a vision, which instructed him to travel to the East and thereafter, travelled extensively in Turkey, Syria, as well as making the pilgrimage to Mecca. In 1223, he settled in Damascus, where he taught, wrote and gathered a circle of disciples. It was there that he died in 1240.

He gave to Sufism a philosophical basis. Earlier Sufi writings were mostly practical guides for followers of the Path or attempted descriptions of the mystical states, which the author had experienced. Ibn 'Arabi formulated the doctrines of Islamic mysticism and set down his 'unveilings, witnessings, and tastings' for all to read.

Ibn 'Arabi was an amazingly prolific author. Some 850 works have been attributed to him, of which the most famous was 'The Ringstones of the Wisdoms' *Fusus al-hikam*. The basic Sufi teaching, according to Ibn 'Arabi, is of the transcendent unity of Being. This means that although God is absolutely transcendent, the Universe is not entirely separated from God. The Universe is mysteriously plunged in God. To treat anything in the world as independent of God is to be guilty of idolatry. The Sufi aim is union with the Divine, which comes as a result of the love created in human beings for Divine Beauty. Such union is gradually attained by a disciplined moral life and the purification of the heart.

Ibn 'Arabi taught the unity of the inner contents of all religions. He came to see that to have lived one religion fully is to have lived them all, as he wrote in these beautiful words:

My heart has become capable of every form:
it is a pasture for gazelles and
A convent for Christian monks,
And a temple for idols
And the pilgrims' Ka'ba

And the tables of the Torah,
Aand the book of the Qur'an.
I follow the religion of Love:
Whatever way Love's camels take,
That is my religion and my faith.

The same universalism is to be found in the teachings of of Jalal-ad-Din ar-Rumi - also known as Mawlana or Mevlana - (1207-12703)), which means 'Our Master.' He wrote:

The religion of love is apart from all religions:
For lovers (the only) religion and creed is God.

Again,

Not Christian or Jew or Muslim
Not Hindu, Buddhist, Sufi or Zen
Not any religion or cultural system.
I am not from the east or the west...
I belong to the beloved
And have seen the two

Jalal-ad-Din was born in Balkh, which is now in North Afghanistan. In 1219, when he was twelve, the family left Balkh because their home city was threatened by invading Mongols. After a pilgrimage to Mecca, the family eventually ended up in Rum (Anatolia) – hence his surname Rumi, by which he is often called.

Rumi's life and work really divide into three distinct stages. During the first, he was a student of theology and then a teacher. All this was changed by his meeting with a wandering dervish called Shams ad-Dinin in 1244. Now, Rumi discovered the ecstasy of mysticism and spent his time dancing and listening to music. After Shams' disappearance, when he was supported by his friendship with Salah ad-Din Zarkub, he wrote the *Divan–i-Shams (The Collected Poetry of Shams)*. During, the third period, following Zarkub's death, he was inspired by another disciple Husam ad-Din Chelebi. His great work the *Mathnawi* is called 'the book of Husam.' Rumi died on 17th December 1273 on what is known as his 'wedding night', when he was finally united with God.

There are various accounts of Rumi's meeting. with Shams, who asked 'What is the purpose of wisdom and knowledge?' 'To follow and reach the Prophet,' Rumi replied. 'That is common place' Shams responded. 'What then is the purpose of knowledge?' Rumi asked. 'Knowledge is that which takes you to its source,' was Shams' answer. The difference is between knowing *about* God – theology - and knowing God – mysticism. Rumi, subsequently in his verses, makes clear the limitation of intellectual activity.

If in the world you are the most learned scholar of the time,
Behold the passing away of this world and this time.

Under Shams' guidance, Rumi experienced the ecstasy of union with God. Having previously disapproved of music, now, in the words of his son, 'day and night he danced in ecstasy, raving like a madman.' His students were horrified and jealous of Shams, who according to some accounts was stabbed by one of his enemies. Rumi was devastated and at first refused to accept that Shams had died and expressed his grief in the poem, *Divan* - a collection of about 25,000 rhyming couplets. Rumi's equally lengthy and most famous work, the *Mathnawi*, composed while he was performing whirling dances, was dictated over nearly twelve years to Husam.

The overwhelming emphasis of Rumi's writing is on the wonder of divine and human love.

Love is not contained in speech and hearing:
Love is an ocean whereof the depth is invisible.'

After Rumi's death, his son, Sultan Walad, who wrote his biography organised his followers into a loose fraternity, known as Mawlawiyya or Mevlevi Order, a name derived' from one of the titles given to Rumi. In the West, the Order is usually known as the Whirling Dervishes. The Order gained great importance during the Ottoman Empire, but Ataturk, the modernising ruler of Turkey, banned all dervish orders in 1925. Visitors to Konya, however, besides visiting his tomb, can now observe the dances at what are, supposedly, cultural programmes.

The Sufi tradition presents another face of Islam to that shown by the suicide bomber. Which is the true Islam? What is true religion?

Chapter 10. ADAPTING TO THE MODERN WORLD

Modern challenges to religions

The last two hundred years have seen enormous challenges to all religions. Intellectually, Darwin, Freud, Marx, Nietzsche and the development of modern scientific ways of thinking have transformed the way many of us see the world and man and woman's place in it. Critical study of religious texts has implied that these are human creations rather than divine revelations. Politically, two of the major ideologies which dominated the twentieth century, Fascism and Communism, were anti-religious. Technologically, patterns of life have changed dramatically in the more affluent parts of the world. Globalisation is imposing a competitive capitalist economy on traditional societies and turning local cultures into tourist attractions.

Religion, as we have suggested, especially in the West, has been pushed to some extent to the margins of life, although the secular society of which many people spoke so confidently in the sixties and seventies is now more questionable. Secularism, as we have seen, is a word used to cover several phenomena. It implies the autonomy of daily life. In a secular society individual citizens do not have any moral pattern of behaviour imposed upon them by the state. For example in many Western countries homosexual acts, which were until quite recently illegal and punishable by law, are now considered a private matter for consenting individuals. In the same way, in many countries, abortion, with certain restrictions, is no longer illegal. In a secular society religion has no place in government and in political and economic life - although in practice the matter is not so clear cut. Thus in the USA, there is a clear separation of church and state: but a President will often end a speech with the words, 'God bless America.' To the Western visitor religion seems much in evidence in India, but constitutionally it is a secular state in the sense that no religion is meant to be given favoured treatment, although all should be treated with respect. In both England and Scotland there are established churches, but their influence is waning fast.

Secularism may also describe a change of mood by which people no longer seek to explain life by reference to religious beliefs. Instead, they will look for a natural rather than a divine cause of illness or disaster. Some sociologists of religion suggest that in the West religion should be regarded as a private or even a 'leisure time' activity. This, of course, is not a view that a committed Christian would accept and is even more alien to the devout Muslim, who, if he or she has been brought up to think of Britain or America as 'Christian' countries, is puzzled by what seems to him or her their moral decadence, especially in terms of permissive sexuality and drug-taking.

In addition to these challenges, which all religions have had to face, much of the Islamic world has had to cope with Western imperialism and now with the political, economic and military dominance of the super-powers, and particularly of the USA. Moreover, many of the challenges to religion mentioned above were cradled in Western society. This means that for some Muslims the West is cause of all their problems.

In very broad terms, there are two reactions of Muslims to the changing world. One is to search for a *modus vivendi* whereby Muslims, true to their faith, participate fully in Western society. The other is confrontational. We shall look in this chapter at some representative figures, who,in different ways, have shown how Muslims might adapt to modern life. In the next chapter, we shall look at some leaders who are hostile to the West. (It is, I recognise, misleading, if helpful to equate the West and the modern world.) This also is not the place for a detailed analysis of the situation in particular countries. It is also hard to generalise about two centuries and large areas of the world. Individual Muslim countries are each different.

The responses of religious people to change may be distinguished in terms of those who uphold the tradition and seek to show its universal relevance; those who try to adapt practices to fit in with contemporary culture and those who are loyal to their faith but are also at home in the modern world.

Upholding the Tradition

The scholar Akbar Ahmed, who has taught in America and Britain, in his *Post-Modernism and Islam*, includes amongst those who maintain the tradition, Ismail Faruqi and Hossein Nasr. Both are faithful to Islam but equally at home in Western and Eastern thought and indeed 'citizens of the world.' Through the World Congress of Faiths I had the privilege of meeting both Ismail Faruqi, who has been quoted several times, and also Hossein Nasr.

Isma'il Raji al-Faruqi (1921–1986) was a Palestinian-American philosopher, who spent several years at Al-Azhar University in Cairo and then taught at universities in North America, including Temple University, where he founded and chaired the Islamic Studies programme. Dr al-Faruqi was also the founder of the International Institute of Islamic Thought. He vigorously defended orthodox Muslim teaching but in the language and thought-forms of contemporary Western scholarship He was committed to inter-relious dialogue, but critical of the approach to this of many Western scholars. He was an activist who sought to transform the Islamic community at home and abroad.

Al-Faruqi and his wife, Lois Lamya al-Faruqi, were stabbed to death in their home in Wyncote, Pennsylvania on May 27, 1986.

Seyyed Hossein Nasr (b.1933), who is currently University Professor of Islamic Studies at the George Washington University, is another outstanding scholar, deeply influenced by Sufism, who is entirely at home in contemporary scholarship and at the same time faithful to the best traditions of Islam. He grew up in Persia and was a professor at Tehran University, before fleeing to America to escape the Iranian revolution in 1979.

Besides his extremely active intellectual life, he spends much time in prayer, meditation and contemplation and provides spiritual counsel for those who seek his advice and guidance. It has been said of him that he has found his home in the inviolable and sacred Center which is neither in the East nor the West.

Adapting to the Outside World

Others have sought to adapt traditional beliefs and practices to the prevalent outlook and assumptions of the wider contemporary society. Two examples of the latter from the nineteenth and early twentieth centuries are Sir Sayyed Ahmed Khan, who established the Muhammadan Anglo-Oriental College at Aligarh, which was consciously modelled on Oxbridge, and Sir Muhammad Iqbal (1876-1938), on whom I will concentrate.

Iqbal tried to reinterpret Islam in the light of the Sufi heritage and Western philosophy, especially the evolutionary thought of the French philosopher Henri Bergson (1859-1941), who is best known for his books *Creative Evolution* and *Creative Mind*. The key feature of Iqbal's thought was the notion of reality as pure duration, with God and human beings interrelating dynamically in the universe. He believed that the marriage of intellect and love could transform human beings into a higher level of being. Iqbal's constant theme was 'Arise, and create a new world'. His poetry in Urdu and Persian inspired Indian Muslims in the first half of the twentieth century to shape and improve their condition of life and was a factor behind the creation of Pakistan. In his *Reconstruction of Religious Thought in Islam* (1928), Iqbal gave a more systematic elaboration of his Islamic vision, arguing for a return to independent judgement, *ijtihad,* and the establishment of a legislative institution for the reformation of Islamic law. S.A Husain, an Indian Muslim professor of philosophy, drawing attention to the word 'reconstruction' rather than 're-interpretation' said that Iqbal 'while he seems to be elaborating the meaning of a verse of the Qur'an, is really using it as a peg to hang his own ideas on.'

Wilfred Cantwell Smith, who taught in Pakistan and later became Professor of the History of Comparative Religion at Harvard, wrote, in a book published in the middle of the last century,

'Today if Islam would function in this radically new world in which we find ourselves, it must be refashioned to give dynamic initiative and vision to man facing a life of opportunity and to give him creative love towards the community of his fellow men. Such a refashioning was a service rendered to Islam chiefly by the outstanding Muslim poet and thinker of the century, Muhammad Iqbal.'

Cantwell Smith's comment, which he might well have revised later in his life, is interesting for the assumption, common at the time that he wrote it, that liberal re-interpretation must be the way forward for religion in the modern world. As a long standing member of the Modern Church People's Union, I sympathise with this, but it is not the dominant mood in Islam today, although Iqbal's influence is not forgotten.

Others in this category are those whom Akbar Ahmed describes as 'modernist.' By this he means contemporary writers, of whom the common feature is, 'the general belief that religion as a force or guide is no longer valid in our age.' He mentions, as examples, two writers who have been influenced by Marxism. One is Tariq Ali, (b 1943), who was born in Pakistan and now lives in Britain. He has been described as 'a military historian, novelist, journalist, filmmaker, public intellectual, political campaigner, activist,. The other is the and the novelist Salman Rushdie, (b.1947) who is best known for his book *The Satanic Verses.*

On the right, he refers to Shahid Burki and Rana Kabbani. Shahid Burki was born in Simla in 1938 and moved to Pakistan after partition. He joined the World Bank in 1974 and became a Vice-President. He took a leave of absence from the World Bank to serve as Pakistan's Finance Minister in 1996-1997. He is the author of a number of books He retired from the Bank in 1999.

Rana Kabbani, who would now be better described as a traditionalist, was born in Damascus in 1958. She is a Syrian writer and broadcaster who lives in London. She has been a vocal critic of the President Assad's regime. In her *Imperial Fictions: Europe's Myths of Orient* she evaluated Western perceptions of Islamic culture with particular reference to the formulation of erotic stereotypes in literature and painting. The increase in hostility towards Islam produced by events following the publication of Salman Rushdie's *The Satanic Verses* prompted Kabbani to clarify the religious and cultural character of the Muslim world in *A Letter to Christendom* (1989). In this impassioned letter to the West, she led the reader through the labyrinthine world of Islam. She described the historical record of western prejudice against Muslims as well as her own experience of life in the West. In so doing, she showed that deep misunderstanding and fear continue to inform the way Islam is perceived today. With particular reference to the Salman Rushdie affair, she illustrated how quickly the old forms of hatred and bigotry surface in order to wage contemporary political battles. She also made a plea for a new dialogue, free from historical bias or personal animosity, between these two civilizations

Being Confident Muslims at Home in the Modern World

Far more common than modernists are those who are concerned to reform abuse or corruption, but who in no way wish to question the message of Islam. They are confident that Muslims can live true to their faith and also be at home in the modern world. Reform, of course, can be quite superficial but it can be far reaching.

I take as examples: Maulana Wahiduddin Kahn, who is a member of the Indian Muslim minority; Farid Esack, who is from South Africa, where again Muslims are in a minority; Zaki Badawi, an outstanding leader of British Muslims and Chandra Muzaffar a leading reformer and activist in Malaysia.

Maulana Wahiduddin Kahn 'stands out as a voice in the wilderness,' said Dr Yoginder Sikand, in a paper I heard at a conference at the Punjabi University in Patiala. Kahn called for an understanding of Islam that is both rooted in the original sources of Islam, while at the same time willing wholeheartedly, although critically, to engage with modernity, responding positively to serious concerns such as questions of peace, inter-religious dialogue and political activism.'

Maulana Wahiduddin Kahn was born in what is now Uttar Pradesh in 1925. At first he joined the Jama'at-i-Islami Hind, which was founded by Abul 'Ala Maududi. Kahn was searching for a socially engaged spirituality, but he came to see that the agenda of the Jama'at, which was working for the establishment of an Islamic state in India, was impractical. He moved for a time to the Tablighi Jama'at, but by 1975 he had cut his links with it because of its hostility to the creative application of Islamic law to the challenges of changing social conditions. In 1976 Khan set up his own research centre in New Delhi. He believed that a new understanding of Islam was necessary to appeal to modern educated Indians.

Khan accepts that Muslims in India are and are likely to remain a minority. They need to seek a solution to their problems by internal reform rather than by conflict with the state or the dominant Hindu majority. He takes seriously the issue of pluralism and inter-community relations and stresses the need to build bridges with people of other faiths. He quotes from the Qur'an the saying 'Unto you your religion and unto me mine.'(109, 6). Islam enjoins Muslims to live with others as brothers in spirit. Khan argues that the Muslims of India today find themselves in a position similar to that of the Prophet and his followers in Mecca, when the nascent community was small and relatively powerless. Just as the Prophet at that time concentrated on peaceful preaching so Muslims in India today should do the same. They should also concern themselves with the problems and issues of the whole country instead of just thinking about their own communal interests.

Khan suggests that the traditional distinction between the 'house of Islam' or lands ruled by Muslims, *dar-ul islam,* and lands ruled by non-Mulsims, traditionally known as *dar-ul harb* or 'the house of war' needs to be rethought. The term 'house of war' only applied to those lands where Muslims were persecuted for their faith and had to resort to violence in self-defence. There should be a third category, which he calls the 'house of invitation' or *dar-ul da'wah,* to refer to lands under non-Muslim control but where Muslims are welcome and have full civil rights. Here the Muslim responsibility is to address non-Muslims with the message of Islam but not to seek confrontation. A similar view was expressed when a delegation from the World Muslim League visited Oxford in March 2002. In answer to a question Dr Abdullah of the League said that the distinction between the 'house of war' and the 'house of Islam' was a historical concept which does not apply today. He stressed that Muslims in Britain should see themselves as good British citizens.

Maulana Wahiduddin Khan also insists that non-Muslims should not be spoken of as *kafirs*. To do so is 'to violate God's injunctions.' The term *kafir* should only be applied to someone who knowingly rejects or conceals the truth. Khan has not created a 'movement' and he has been attacked for collusion with the 'enemies of Islam.'

Farid Esack (b. 1959), who studied for a time in Britain, is a leading South African scholar and activist. Reference has already been made to his book *On Being A Muslim*. This and another book, *Qur'an, Liberation and Pluralism*, are both written in the context of the struggle in South Africa against apartheid - a struggle with which many Muslims, including Esack, identified. This struggle led Farid Esack to reflect on key Qur'anic passages used in the context of oppression to rethink the role of Islam in a plural society. He shows how traditional interpretations of the Qur'an were used to legitimise an unjust order, but that these same texts, if interpreted within a contemporary socio-historical context, support active solidarity with people of other religions in the struggle for change. In describing the objectives of his book, Esack puts first the wish 'to show that it is possible to live in faithfulness to both the Qur'an and to one's present context alongside people of other faiths, working with them to establish a more humane society.' Towards the end of the book, Esack refers to a Call of Islam publication *Women Arise! The Qur'an Liberates You,* which says that 'we must unleash a debate on the question of women so that equality and freedom become achievable.' But the document hastens to add that 'this debate need not depart from the pages of the Qur'an at all for within these pages there is sufficient evidence to suggest that Muslim women can and must play a full role in our society.'

Sheik Zaki Badawi (1922-2006) was another visionary scholar who helped British Islam make peace with modernity. He was born in Egypt and was educated at the University of Al-Azhar in Cairo, where he became a celebrated scholar and professor there, but made his home in Britain in 1976 where he died suddenly in 2006. In 1978 he was appointed as the first chief imam at Regent's Park mosque, in London, He said that his mission was to save British Islam from dangerous isolation. 'I was horrified that none of the other imams could speak English,' he recalled. 'I was amazed that they didn't understand anything about other religions and were so unfamiliar with western culture.'

Zaki Badawi, who wrote the Preface for the first edition of this book, was Britain's most influential Muslim. Prince Charles paid a warm tribute to him at a memorial gathering after his death. Badawi spent nearly 30 years almost single handedly creating British Islamic institutions and setting out arguments in their favour. Thus he laid the intellectual and bureaucratic foundations for that community as a growing minority to become full members of British society and contribute to its life. He himself became a well-known public figure, often consulted by the government. As chairman of the Council of Imams and Mosques, which he initiated in 1984 and as principal of the Muslim College, which he founded in 1986, to trains imams for British mosques, he used his position to question constantly the assumptions of the prejudiced: namely that Islam is characterised by violence and primitive practices often oppressive of women, and that it is on a collision course with western values.

To the first charge, Badawi would quote the farewell sermon of the Prophet Muhammad at the foot of the Mount of Mercy: "God had made inviolable for you each other's blood and each other's property until you meet your Lord." He campaigned vigorously in favour of women's rights and, most particularly, against forced marriage and female circumcision, which he considered to be an African custom erroneously inserted into religious tradition in some parts of the Islamic world.

Badawi was an enthusiastic leader of inter-faith dialogue. With Sir Sigmund Sternberg and myself, he founded the Three Faiths Forum in 1997. He highlighted Islam's history of flexibility and tolerance - particularly of Judaism - speaking of the common Abrahamic roots and Hellenistic heritage of Islam and Christianity. "Their ethical principles are not in conflict," he would say. "Past and even present conflicts between them originate in territorial ambitions and over the acquisition of resources."

At crucial moments of tension, Badawi used his considerable learning and authority to steer British Islam (he coined the term) on a wise course. He immediately condemned the 9/11 atrocity as "a violation of Islamic law and ethics". When, in 1989, other Islamic figures threatened Salman Rushdie with death for his novel *The Satanic Verses*, Badawi called on Muslims to spurn the book but spare the man, and declared that he would not hesitate to offer the novelist sanctuary in his home. As the media highlighted fears that British Muslim soldiers would not fight in Iraq, he urged Muslims to obey orders and accurately predicted that there would be no problem of divided loyalty. He also worked hard to make no-interest Islamic mortgages available.

There are other examples of reformers who could be mentioned, such as Chandra Muzaffar (b. 1947) who is a Malaysian Muslim political scientist, and an Islamic reformist and activist. He has written on civilisational dialogue, human rights,

Malaysian politics and international relations. He is now President of the International Movement for a Just World, which seeks to raise public consciousness on the moral and intellectual basis. He is also a member of the Peace Council where I have got to know him

The reformers mentioned above are all are also involved in inter-faith activity. For those to whom the application of faith to the search for peace and social justice is a high priority, it is natural to look for allies among people of other faiths who share this passion.

It could be said of all in this section that, like Zaki Badawi, whose influence stretched far beyond Britain, their aim was to show how Muslims can live at ease in a western liberal environment and to demonstrate that the gulf between east and west, ancient and modern, could be bridged peacefully and fruitfully.

Chapter 12.CONFRONTING WESTERN GLOBALIZATION

For a significant number of Muslims the answer to the challenges of the modern world to Islam is to resist them - sometimes, for a small minority, with force. They may welcome technological advance and scientific discovery, but reject many of the assumptions of secular society. Many Muslims still live as their parents did and continue to practice the religion in which they were brought up without much awareness of the challenges to it posed by modern society. The people mentioned in this chapter are fully aware of the challenges and are determined to oppose them

The Wahhabiya movement

One example is the Wahhabiya movement, partly because of its influence, which Muhammad ibn Abd al-Wahhab (1703-87) initiated in the Arabian peninsula during the eighteenth century, an ultra-conservative puritanical movement which adhered to Hanbalite *shari'a* - the most literal and dogmatic interpretation of the law - which rejected centuries of legal interpretation as well as the mysticism of the Sufis. Al-Wahhab found a champion in the tribal leader Muhammad ibn Sa'ud and the Saudis became the main supporters of the movement. In 1801, the Wahhabis slaughtered two thousand ordinary citizens in the streets of Qarbala, so violence is nothing new to this movement.

Another influential figure was al-Afghani (1838-97), who was born in Iran but who spent his formative years in Afghanistan. He aimed to rally the Muslim world to realise its power as an international community and, by raising its political and intellectual standards, to combat Western colonialism. Freedom from foreign rule was he hoped to be followed by the establishment of a pan-Islamic state and the union of all Muslims under a caliph.

He regarded the Arabic language as of primary importance in promoting Muslim unity. His programme, he believed, would lead to improvements in the living standards of all Muslims. He affirmed the transcendental truth of Islam in his *The Refutation of the Materialists*. Towards the end of his life, he was hunted down by the Iranian authorities, but although three of his colleagues were hanged, he himself died of cancer.

The Muslim Brotherhood

In the early part of the twentieth century, the Muslim struggle against the West turned into a mass movement. In 1928 an Egyptian called al-Banna (1906-49) founded the Muslim Brotherhood, al-Ikhwan al-Muslimun, which rapidly gained support across the Middle East. Banna, who like many other radicals was a middle class intellectual, was in sympathy with the ideas of Afghani and deplored the disunity and moral laxity of Egyptian society, which he blamed on British occupation. One day, he wrote, six labourers from a British camp came to see him and said:

'We are weary of this life of humiliation and restriction. Lo, we see that Arabs and the Muslims have no status and no dignity. They are not more than mere hirelings belonging to the foreigners. We possess nothing but this blood... and these souls ... and these few coins... We are unable to perceive the road to action as you perceive it, or to know the path to the service of the fatherland, the religion and the nation as you know it. All that we desire now is to present you with all we possess, to be acquitted by God of the responsibility, and for you to be responsible before Him for us and for what we must do.'

So the Muslim Brotherhood was born. By 1949, it had 2,000 branches and some half million members. Banna told his followers in 1943, 'You are not a benevolent society, nor a political party, nor a local organisation having limited purposes. Rather, you are a new soul in the heart of the nation to give it life by means of the Qur'an.'

Banna's aim was to free Egypt from British control and to establish an Islamic state, eliminating such Western influences as night-clubs, casinos and pornography. After the Second World War, al-Banna took up the cause of the Palestinians, but his activities were restricted by the Egyptian government. At the end of 1948, many members of the Muslim Brotherhood were arrested. Soon afterwards a young member of the movement shot and killed the prime minister of Egypt, Nuqrashi Pasha and seven weeks later Hasan al-Banna was himself assassinated by secret servant agents.

Banna's death was a serious blow to the Brotherhood, although the writings of Sayyid Qutb, who was executed in 1966, had considerable influence. His widely read *Malim fi al-Tariq* argued that social systems were of two types. Either there was a Nizam Islami - a true Islamic order - or a Nizam Jahli, that is the rule of pre-Islamic ignorance. As Egypt did not belong to the first category, it belonged to the second and therefore it was the duty of true Muslims to wage jihad against ignorant and despotic governments. In passing it is worth emphasising that radical Muslims are often as critical of many Muslim governments, which they consider in the pay of the West, as they are of Western powers themselves. Members of the Muslim Brotherhood described Egypt's defeat in the Six-Day War 'as a sign of God's punishment for leaving the path of Islam.' They too were responsible for the assassination of President Sadat, whom they accused of treachery against Islam and the Palestinian people by his agreement to the Camp David Accord.

Following the overthrow of President Mubarak, the Muslim Brotherhood has become a powerful and force and governing party in Egypt, creating concern amongst some of the leaders of the uprising that Egypt will become an Islamic state rather than the modern democracy for which they hoped.

Taliban

The most spectacular victories for militant Islam have been the Iranian revolution in 1979 and the capture of Kabul by the Taliban in 1979. The Shah of Iran and his father had tried to westernise their country. Traditional Muslim styles of dress were banned and western education promoted. Opponents ran foul of the much feared secret police. When Muslim clergy protested, the Shah dismissed them as 'black reactionaries'. He expelled the most vociferous protester, Ayatollah Khomeini (1902-89), a leader of the Twelver Shi'ite Muslims. In exile, he became more dangerous and eventually succeeded in overthrowing the Shah in 1979. As leader of the revolution, he purged Iran of Western influences. His *fatwa* or ban against Salman Rushdie's *The Satanic Verses*, which he regarded as blasphemous, was widely accepted in the Muslim world.

The Taliban was originally a military group, formed in response to the invasion of Afghanistan by the Soviet Union. As part of the Cold War against the Soviet Union, both America and Britain trained Taliban fighters in guerrilla warfare and supplied arms and money. When they gained power, members of the Taliban showed themselves even more rigorous than Ayatollah Khomeini in imposing a version of Islamic law, which most Muslims regard as crude and distorted.

Recent years have also seen a revival of the original militant movement founded by al-Wahhab with a network of organisations, under various names. These groups have been involved in prolonged struggles in Algeria, where the Islamic party won a general election but were denied power and where there have been atrocities on both sides. Militants are said to be responsible for the deaths of seventy tourists at Luxor in 1997 and to be linked with armed groups in Kashmir.

al-Qaida

The most notorious group is, of course, al-Qaida, led by Osama bin-Laden, which was responsible for the devastating attack on the Twin Towers in New York on September 11th, 2001 - an event that has over shadowed world history for the last decade. It was the direct cause of the Second Gulf War against Saddam Hussein's regime in Iraq and the invasion of Afghanistan by American and British troops who hoped to destroy a-Qaida hide-outs in that country. The Taliban became the most determined opposition to American and British forces.

It must be emphasised that the great majority of Muslims want nothing to do with violence and most have condemned the terrorist attacks on America. Even so, it is important to hear what some of these militants are saying so as to see how the world is seen through the eyes of the most alienated Muslims. Terror draws its sustenance from disaffection which is caused by the hopelessness of those who feel victimised by poverty and injustice.

Ayatollah Khomaini was a long standing critic of the Shah of Persia's regime, but during his exile, he broadened his opposition to attack the institution of monarchy itself and to call not just for adherence to Islamic law, but for the establishment of an Islamic state. In about 1969 he gave a series of lectures to his students, which were published as a book entitled *Velayat-e Faqih*. There are four main themes. First the book condemns the institution of monarchy as alien to Islam, abhorrent to the Prophet and the source of all Iran's misfortunes over 2,500 years. Secondly, it is a blue-print for an Islamic state. This is based on the message of the Qur'an and exemplified by the Islamic community led by the Prophet in the seventh century. Ayatollah Khomaini regarded this as a practical form of government realisable in the lifetime of the present generation and not just as some distant ideal. Thirdly, and this is particular to the Shi'ite tradition, the claim of the clerical class, as heirs of the Prophet, to the leadership of the community is forcefully asserted. Justice and an expertise in Islamic law are essential for those who rule. 'The real governors', he says, 'are the Islamic jurists themselves.' Although leadership is vested collectively in the religious leadership (*ulama*), it can be vested in a single leader. Fourthly, *Velayat-e Faqi* calls on all believers to work actively for the overthrow of the non-Islamic state. 'We have no choice', Khomaini wrote, 'but to shun wickedness, and to overthrow governors who are traitorous, wicked, cruel

117

and tyrannical.' He urged revolution, but not violence.

The statements of Osama bin-Laden are more directly political in tone. In a 'World Islamic Front Statement' entitled 'Jihad Against Jews and Crusaders', Osama bin-Laden argued that the United States of America had created a state of war against the Muslim world and in particular the people of the Arabian Peninsula. He spoke of the occupation of the Arabian Peninsula, which contains Islam's most holy places, and argued that it was being used by the Americans as a staging post for continuing aggression against the Iraqi people, of whom he claimed more than one million had been killed. Further giving his backing to the Palestinian Hamas party, he complained of the 'occupation of Jerusalem and the murder of Muslims there' - Israel, being seen as an American puppet state. These American actions, in his view, amounted to a 'clear declaration of war on God, his messenger, and Muslims.' Further because the *ulema* have throughout Islamic history unanimously agreed that the *jihad* is an individual duty if the enemy destroys Muslim countries', Osama bin-Laden, therefore, declared that it was a duty for every Muslim to try to kill Americans and their allies. He quoted verses from the Qur'an (2, 193 and 4, 75) to justify this call.

Muslim Resentment

This is an extreme position, which I in no way seek to justify, but if there is to be an alternative to violent reaction to violence, then at least we need to hear the complaint of those who sympathise with Osama bin-Laden's attack on America and the West. Some years ago, not for the first time, I visited a Palestinian Refugee camp. An elderly woman told us how her whole life had been spent in being moved from one refugee camp to yet another refugee camp. In the bitterness and despair of those we talked to, I felt more than ever their deep sense of injustice and of a wasted life - a sense of injustice felt by most Muslims. There is bitterness too about the failure of Western powers to protect the Bosnian Muslims or to curb the ruthless Russian suppression of Chechnyan rebels. Terrorism is not to be condoned and I deplore all violence, but in every age victims of ruthless regimes have been driven to armed resistance. One person's terrorist is another person's freedom-fighter.

There is also a sense amongst some Muslims that Western concern for human rights is selective and that the world economic system operates largely to the benefit of the West and those Arab rulers who are in league with them. To some eyes, globalisation is seen as the bed-fellow of modernism. Like Kalim

Siddiqui,(b.1931) for example, who is known for his leadership of the British Muslim Parliament, they see interfaith dialogue as pointless and reject the possibility of a *modus vivendi* with the West.

I do not want to pursue the political analysis, but it is impossible to separate political and religious issues in the present situation. What is felt by many Muslims as injustice contributes to oppositional attitudes and the rejection of all that the West stands for. Raficq Abdullah, a Muslim lawyer who lives in London, wrote in *Muslim-Christian Dialogue, Promise and Problems* that for millions of Muslims who live in poverty and who feel profoundly marginalised, modernity has nothing to offer them. It embodies, he says,

'The virulent return of *jahilliyah* or ungodliness which now infests the whole world including Muslim societies... It is justified by man-made laws which transgress God's legislative authority as enshrined in the religious law or *Shari'a*. This comprehensive failure to abide by the only sovereign law which is God's exclusive attribute and prerogative is the cause of moral decay and spiritual bankruptcy. A true Muslim's only shield against this seemingly intractable threat to his or her identity is a reversion to the authentic experience of Islam as it was practised during the lives of the Prophet and the rightly-guided Caliphs.'

Raficq Abdullah is at pains to make clear that Islam is not a monolithic entity, but adds that the rejection of modernity and the 'West' is shared by both Sunni and Shi'a Islamists. Raficq Abdullah also makes very clear that he does not share these views. He and accuses those who take this position of committing 'epistemological legerdemain by projecting their deeply nostalgic version of events of the founding moment of Islam as ahistorical categories, as givens which it would be sacrilegious, indeed blasphemous, to place under critical scrutiny'.

Islamist

Raficq uses the term 'Islamists.' Some years before 9/11 Professor Khalid Duran, of the Foreign Policy Research Institute in Philadelphia, made a distinction between *Muslims* and *Islamists*. He compares the distinction to that in Germany between *evangelisch* and *evangelikal* ('Protestant' and 'Protestant fundamentalist'). Similarly before the fall of the Berlin Wall both regimes in Germany claimed they were 'democratic'. Two titles which sound almost the same may have sharply different meanings. One Muslim explained the difference by saying that 'Muslims say "God is most great", whereas Islamists say "Islam is most great", although that is rather too simple.

The origins of the Islamic Movement, as we have seen, lie with the Wahhabi movement that emerged in Central Arabia in the eighteenth and nineteenth century. Its aim was to revive the Muslim society of seventh century Madina in its 'pristine purity.' They rejected centuries of legal scholarship and the mystical Sufi tradition. They were 'fundamentalist' in the sense that scriptural statements are not seen in their historical context and are treated as absolute - whereas any revealed statement ought to be open to interpretation. A similar vision inspired Hasan al-Banna, mentioned above, who founded the Muslim Brotherhood Party. He wanted to return to original Islam 'cleansed of all later accretions such as theology, philosophy and mysticism.' Compare this to the motto of Z A Bhutto's Pakistan People's Party: 'Our religion is Islam, our political system is democracy, our economic orientation is socialism' - a slogan that was anathema to Islamists. There is a real ideological struggle in many Muslim countries reflecting radically different understandings of the Muslim religion.

A Struggle for the Soul of Islam

'Islamist', like 'fundamentalist' or 'extremists', is a term I have tried to avoid, because labels often say more about the views of those who use them than about those to whom they are supposed to refer. Labels may be an excuse for not listening to the call for justice of those who feel marginalised. As Raficq Abdullah pointed out, the way in which some in the West speak of all Muslims as if they were terrorists is as unhelpful as the way some Muslims see all Westerners as enemies of the true faith. As Edward Said has observed, 'the real battle is not a clash of civilisations, but a clash of definitions.' The struggle should not be the West against the world of Islam, rather a struggle is going on for the soul of Islam and indeed there is sharp struggle between conservative and liberal questions. Once again, the question is what is true religion?

Most of the Muslims I know and the ones whom we are likely to meet in dialogue are Muslims - in the sense I am using it. They are also usually heirs to the Enlightenment so share many of the assumptions of the modern paradigm. In his book on Judaism, Hans Küng speaks of 'paradigm shifts' and suggests that you can have periods when people of the same faith are living in different paradigm times, which means that they have few shared assumptions about life and the world. Islamists reject 'modernism', partly because their view of life starts from different basic assumptions. So often, disputes about religion arise from historical, social and economic arguments as much as from theological ones.

120

The struggle within Islam is primarily a matter for Muslims, but sympathetic friends need to be aware of the struggle that is taking place, and to be supportive of those Muslims who are willing to take the risk of dialogue. Christians can help to make known the views of the latter group, thereby resisting the stereotyping of Muslims which will make prophecies of a clash of civilisations self-fulfilling. This is also a time when more than ever Christians need to seek dialogue with those Muslims who are willing to take part in it.

It is also vital to help Muslims in Europe and America feel that they are accepted as full citizens and that they have a stake and share in our society. One of the dangers in some urban areas of Britain is that young Muslims not only feel alienated from 'white English society' but are also increasingly alienated from the mosques and the leaders of the Muslim community. Many Muslims are making a major contribution to British life at all levels of our society, as I know partly from attending the Awards for Excellence ceremonies organised by the *Muslim News* or from meeting young Muslims who take part in the programmes of the Three Faiths Forum. Yet others like a young Muslim woman at a check-out in Cowley or a Rhodes scholar at one of the colleges in Oxford have told me that they feel marginalised and have experienced discrimination and racial abuse. The search for a harmonious society in which difference is seen as enrichment should be seen as a responsibility of all faith communities as well as of interfaith organisations

On the international scene, governments, *all* governments have to address the root causes of poverty and injustice - and this includes tackling trade discrimination, the arms trade as well as seeking solutions for long-standing areas of tension in the Middle East and in Kashmir and Sudan. People of faith have constantly to call upon the leaders of the nations to live up to their responsibilities. Even now, the tragic events of September 11th could be a wake-up call to strive for the new world order that some of us hoped for at the start of a new millennium.

CONCLUSION

The dangerous international situation makes urgent demands upon both Christians and Muslims.

Chapter 11. LOOKING AHEAD

Can a 'dialogue of civilisations' replace the 'clash of civilisations? The United Nations now has a programme to promote intercultural and interreligious dialogue. There are at least four ways, I suggest, by which greater understanding between Christians and Muslims could be encouraged.

Reject Isolationism

First, members of each faith need to purge their religion of isolationism and acquiesence in social injustice. This will mean making clear the authentic interpretation of the teachings of the faith, challenging false interpretations, and may mean re-examination of traditional teaching in the current socio-historical context. In this task, the friendly criticism of the other may help members of one faith see how some traditional statements are misunderstood or how past hostilities still cloud our relationship today. The outsider can help us recognise our blind spots

Shared Moral Values

Second, Christians and Muslims need, together with members of other faiths, to reflect on the values that they share and on the moral basis of a healthy society and a just and peaceful international order. They then should work together for the implementation of these values. My good friend, Dr S A Ali, former Chancellor of Hamdard University in New Delhi, expressed this very movingly when he wrote:

> Doctrinal differences should be relegated to the rear and more important issues should be the focus of discussion. What is the meaning of life? What is the position of Islam and Christianity on moral issues like abortion, machine-assisted insemination and euthanasia? What are the social issues of our time and how to solve them? How can terrorism be combated and how to put a stop to the diversion of funds from development to the production of weapons of mass destruction? How to check pollution and improve the quality of life? How to secure for all people on earth basic human rights, freedom from fear and equality and dignity? To do this, and much else, is then the mission and goal of both Christianity and Islam. Should they not, then join hands and change the world scenario, fulfilling Omar Khayyam's dream:

Ah Love Could Thou and I with Fate conspire
To change this sorry scheme of things entire?
Would we not shatter it to bits, and then
Remould it nearer to the heart's desire?

It is a hopeful sign that leaders of public opinion in other spheres of life are now recognising the importance of the moral and spiritual dimension of life in society.

The moral conscience of humanity

Third, to make real change possible, people of different faiths need to be far more proactive in challenging the abuses of government, international institutions and the economic system. They should be the voice of the moral conscience of humanity, pleading for the poor, the dispossessed and the victims of violence. They should act together to protect human rights and the environment. This is beginning to happen, but, paradoxically, the interfaith movement which draws together people of all faiths in the search for peace and justice at the same time often makes its members very critical of the compromises that many faith communities have made with the abuse of power and social injustice

Appreciation of each other's faith

Fourth, Muslims and Christians need a better understanding and appreciation of each other's religions. The work of scholars is this field need to be far more widely known. Some of the issues discussed in this book may at first sight seem rather remote from the current crisis, but I hope they show the wide agreement of both religions on their approach to life. Members of both faiths seek to live in accord with the will of God. There are some disagreements in their understanding of the divine will and more often, as I have suggested, differences of emphasis. In open conversation, the emphases and insights of both faiths can help us to come to a clearer understanding of the truth. We can be a spur to each other in our wish to know and obey God's purposes.

As the Qur'an says:

To each among you
Have we prescribed a Law

And an Open Way.
If Allah had so willed,
He would have made you
A single People, but (His Plan is)
To test you in what
He hath give you: so strive
As in a race in all virtues.
The goal of you all is to Allah
It is He that will show you
The truth of the matters
In which you dispute (5, 48)

Books mentioned in the text:

Ahmed, A S, *Postmodernism and Islam,* Routledge, 1992.

Al Faruqi, Ismail R. *Islam* Argus Communications 1979.

Arberry, A J, *Doctrines of the Sufis,* Cambridge University Press. 1935

Arberry, A, *The Koran Interpreted,* Oxford University Press, 1964.

Ayoub, M, *Redemptive Suffering in Islam,* Mouton Publishers, the Hague, 1978.

Aziz-us-Saud, U, *A Comparative Study of Christianity and Islam,*
    Noor Publishing House, Delhi, 1986.

Bell, Richard, *The Qur'an Translated,* T and T Clark, Edinburgh.

Bowker, J, *Problems of Suffering in Religions of the World,*
    Cambridge University Press, 1970.

Braybrooke, Marcus *Christian-Jewish Dialogue: The Next Steps,*
    SCM Press 2000,

Braybrooke, Marcus *Faith and Interfaith in A Global Age,*
    CoNexus and Braybrooke Press, 1998,

Bryant, M Darrol and Ali, S A, *Muslim-Christian Dialogue: Promise and
    Problems,* Paragon House, St Paul, MA, 1998

Christians and Muslims in the Commonwealth, Altajir World of Islam Trust,
    2001

Cragg, Kenneth, *Readings in the Qur'an,* Collins, 1998.

Cragg, Kenneth, *Muhammad and the Christian ,* Darton Longman and Todd.
    1984,

Denzinger, *The Church Teaches, Documents of the Church in English
    Translation,* B Herder Book Co., 1955, p. 165.

Esack, F, *Qur'an, Liberation and Pluralism* Oneworld, 1997.

Esack, F, *On Being a Muslim,* Oneworld, 1999

Hellwig, Monika 'From Christ to God: The Christian Perspective' in *Jews and
    Christians Speak of Jesus,* Ed Arthur E Zannoni, Fortress Press 1994

Hourani, A, *Islam in European Thought,* Cambridge University Press 1991.

Husain, S A, *Islam,* Punjabi University, Patiala, 1969.

Hussein, Kamel, *City of Wrong,* ET Kenneth Cragg, Amsterdam 1959,
    London 1960.

Ibn (al-)Arabi in *Tarjuman al-Ashwaq,* E.T. by R A Nicholson

Khalid, K M *Together on the Road, Muhammad and Jesus,* Cairo,.n.d.

Khan, I A, *Insight Into the Qur'an: Reflections Upon Divine Signs,*
    Genuine Publications and Media, New Delhi 1999

Khan Muhammad Zafrulla, *Muhammad: Seal of the Prophets,* Routledge
    and Kegan Paul 1980,

Lings, M, *Muhammad,* George Allen and Unwin, 1983.
Mitchell, R P, *The Society of the Muslim Brothers,* London, 1969
Mortimer, Edward *Faith and Power in the Politics of Islam,* Faber and Faber 1982,
Muhaiyaddeen, Muhammad Raheem Bawa, *Islam and World Peace,* The Fellowship Press, Philadelphia, PA 19131, 1987.
Nasr, Seyyed Hossein, *Living Sufism,* Unwin, 1972
Nielsen, N C, *Fundamentalism, Mythos and World Religions,* State University of New York Press, 1993.
Noibi, Daud O S, 'O People of the Book: The Qur'an's Approach to Interfaith Co-operation'. a paper given at the New Delhi Colloquium of the Inter-Religious Federation for World Peace.
Otto R, *The Idea of the Holy,* (1917) Penguin, 1959.
Padwick, C, *Muslim Devotions,* SPCK, 1961
Parrinder, E. G, *Jesus in the Qur'an,* Sheldon 1976,
Parto, S., *Seven Faces,* Teheran, n.d..
Pilgrimage to Mecca, General Directorate of Press of the Kingdom of Saudi Arabia. N.d.
Quasem, M A, *The Recitation and Interpretation of the Qur'an,* Bagi, Selangor, Malaysia. 1979.
Repentance: A Comparative Perspective, ed. Etzioni, A and Carney, D E, Rowman and Littlefield Publishers, 1997
Robinson, N, *Discovering the Qur'an,* SCM Press, 1996.
Sajid, Abduljalil 'The Islamic View of Jesus', Pamphlet published by Brighton Islamic Mission, n.d..
Schimmel, A, *And Muhammed is his Messenger,* University of South Carolina Press, 1995
Smith, W Cantwell, *What is Scripture?* SCM Press, 1993.
Tutu, D, *No Future Without Forgiveness,* Rider 1999.
Vahiduddin, S, *What Christ Means to Me.* unpublished paper.
Wahiduddin Khan, *Islam and Peace,* al-Risala, New Delhi, 1999
Watt, W Montgomery, *Islam and Christianity Today,* Routledge and Kegan Paul 1983.
Watt, W Montgomery, *Islamic Fundamentalism and Modernity,* Routledge, 1988
Zakaria, R, *Muhammad and the Qur'an,* Penguin 1991.
Most quotations from the Qur'an are from the English translation by Yusuf Ali as revised and edited by the Presidency of Islamic Researches of Saudi Arabia.

MARCUS BRAYBROOKE

Marcus Braybrooke is a parish priest, who has also been active in interfaith work for many years and is the author of over forty books. Marcus is married to Mary, who is a social worker and a magistrate and who has shared in the parochial ministry and the interfaith work. They have a son and a daughter and six grand-daughters and a poodle, called Toffee.

Marcus Braybrooke has ministered in Highgate in London; Frindsbury in Kent; in Swainswick, Wells and Bath in Somerset; and in the Baldons in Oxfordshire. He is now an honorary assistant priest in the Dorchester-on-Thames Team Ministry in Oxfordshire.

After gaining a degree in history and theology at Cambridge, Marcus studied for a year at Madras Christian College and then at Wells Theological College.

Marcus has been involved in interfaith work for over forty years, especially through the World Congress of Faiths, which he joined in 1964 and of which he is now President. He is a Co-Founder of the Three Faiths Forum and has taught at the Muslim College in London. He is also a Peace Councillor and was one of the founders of the International Interfaith Centre in Oxford.

He has travelled widely to attend interfaith conferences and to lecture. He and Mary have participated in all the modern Parliaments of World Religions

In 2004 Marcus was awarded a Lambeth degree by the Archbishop of Canterbury 'in recognition of his contribution to the development of inter-religious co-operation and understanding throughout the world.'

BOOKS BY MARCUS BRAYBROOKE

Together to the Truth 1971
The Undiscovered Christ of Hinduism 1973
Interfaith worship 1974
Time to Meet 1990
Wide Embracing Love 1990
Children of One God: A History of the Council of Christians and Jews 1991
Pilgrimage of Hope: One Hundred Years of Global Interfaith Dialogue 1992
Stepping Stones to a Global Ethic 1992
Be Reconciled 1992
Dialogue with a Difference (Ed with Tony Bayfield), 1992
Love without Limit 1995
Faith in a Global Age 1995
How to Understand Judaism 1995
A Wider Vision; a history of the World Congress of Faiths 1996
The Wisdom of Jesus
The Miracles of Jesus (with James Harpar), 1997
All in Good Faith (Ed with Jean Potter), 1997
The Explorers' Guide to Christianity 1998
Testing the Global Ethic (Ed with Peggy Morgan), 1998
Christian-Jewish Dialogue: the Next Steps 2000
Learn to Pray 2001
Bridge of Stars (Ed) 2001
What we can learn from Hinduism 2002
What we can learn from Islam 2002
Lifelines (Ed) 2002
One Thousand World Prayers 2003
365 Meditations for a Peaceful Heart and Peaceful World 2004
Sustaining the Common Good (with Kamran Mofid) 2005
A Heart for the World: the Interfaith Alternative 2006
365 Meditations and Inspirations on Love and Peace 2006
Interfaith Witness in a Changing World 2007
Prayers and Blessings (Ed) 2007
Beacons of the Light: 100 holy people who have shaped the
    Spiritual History of Humanity 2009
Meeting Jews 2010
Hinduism: A Christian Reflection - e-book 2012
Peace in Our Hearts: Peace in Our World.-.e-book 2012
Islam: A Christian Reflection e-book 2012
Christians and Jews Building Bridges e-book 2013
Widening Vision: The World Congress of Faiths and the Growing Interfaith Movement – e-book
2013